Transport in Yorkshire

by

Colin Speakman

Dalesman Publishing Company, Ltd.,
Clapham, via Lancaster.
Yorkshire.
1969

10s. 6d.
(52½ p.)

THE COVER ILLUSTRATIONS: Front:- Three eras of transport at Bingley. In the foreground is Three-Rise Lock on the Leeds and Liverpool canal; in the middle distance a diesel unit on the former Leeds & Bradford Extension Railway from Shipley to Colne; in the background a lorry rumbles along A650, originally the Keighley-Bradford turnpike (David Joy). Back, upper:-A remarkable view of Briggate, Leeds, in the age of the horse tram (supplied by Ledbetter of Leeds). Back, lower:- Yorkshire transport of the future—the proposed Humber road bridge.

The line drawing on the title page by P. D. Stoddart is of the Rosedale mineral railway and depicts a train of ironstone skirting the head of Farndale about 1900. W. R. Lang photographed the contrast in modes of transport shown on this page in 1967; the coach-and-four were about to depart from York Castle for London to celebrate the 125th anniversary of the last regular stage-coach run between the two cities. The maps in the book are by G. C. Dickinson (pages 54, 55), E. Gower (8, 11, 15, 24), E. Jeffrey (16, 46, 88, 89), Judith Joy (32, 47, 61, 72) and P. Lavery, in association with Newcastle University's Department of Geography. (87).

Printed and bound in Great Britain by
FRETWELL & BRIAN LTD.
Silsden, Nr. Keighley, Yorkshire.

Contents

Why Transport?

THIS is not a book for the expert. It is for people like myself, who have an interest in and a love of the Yorkshire countryside, and a wish to understand it more fully. What we call "natural" countryside is a subtle blending of natural and human forces. In order to understand and enjoy a landscape as fully as possible, one has to understand these forces that shape it, giving individuality and a peculiar sense of "place." Nothing of man's creation, with the exception of agriculture and forestry, has changed the landscape as dramatically as the development of transportation. Ten minutes with an ordnance map of any part of Yorkshire, with its criss-crossing of paths, roads, canals and railways, will demonstrate what I mean. It is a gradual, continuous process, still at work.

This book is an attempt to understand that process. Inevitably it is superficial, and too briefly attempts to summarise many complex and specialist fields of transport history, often looking nationally rather than locally to understand how a particular form of transport came to exist. Yet a local example of a well-known national trend can suddenly give vividness to history or a novel, and details of what happened in Yorkshire might help illuminate the whole.

Much local research is still to be done before it is too late; it is clear that many precious relics of real historic interest are through indifference, ignorance and slow decay, being eradicated and destroyed. The industrial revolution began in the north of England—we should be more aware of our heritage. This is a plea for its rediscovery and protection.

My gratitude is due to the many writers whose work and researches I have relied on, but above all to Dr. Arthur Raistrick, that great Yorkshire scholar whose knowledge of Dales history can only be described as encyclopaedic. Also to Miss Lilian Smith and Mr. Fred Andrews for valuable ideas and information. And finally to my wife; as an American author wrote recently, writing is not the best of spectator sports, and without her support in all kinds of small but important ways this little book would never have been written.

1: Ridgeways

THE word "way" suggests so many things. It is a method of doing something; we talk of the easiest, the quickest, and the best way to do things and to get to places. A "way" is an idea rather than a thing. But when many people have the same idea and go the same "way" the idea begins to take a physical form. You can see this if just one or two people have a habit of walking across a field or through a wood. At first there is no noticeable trace, but gradually as weeks become months the grass is worn away, the undergrowth cleared, the soil beaten into a muddy path and stones exposed. If a lot of people go that way over the years it gradually widens into a track. Over centuries it wears deeper—then it is repaired with stones, walled and bridged.

In a curious way paths are a bit like words. When we use a word we are in fact echoing the thought-processes of countless humans who have inhabited these islands from time immemorial. When we talk we add our own tiny mite to that vast complex of experience, language. But paths are sometimes even older than language, and walking along some ancient path we may be retracing the very steps of our remote and long forgotten ancestors, men whose hands and feet helped to shape the landscape. England, and in particular Yorkshire, has a landscape which is like a vast and complex book. Each generation has left its handwriting on the page, one sometimes partially obliterating the other. To read the handwriting of earlier ages needs skill and care, but it is a fascinating study. How from the vast mass of evidence, from the jumble and muddle, the criss-cross of lines and patterns on the map, can one decipher the story? It is a slow process, sometimes tantalisingly difficult, and yet there are many clues.

We know little about our earliest ancestors, although precious fragments of evidence have been used to create a picture of sorts. We know, for instance, that men probably lived in Victoria Cave, Settle, during the Upper Palaeolithic period, around 10,000 B.C., for a few bone impliments from that period have been discovered in the cave. Tests on the remains of a camp at Star Carr, near Seamer, show that a band of primitive hunters lived there about 7,500 B.C. The very first dwellers in what must have been a cold, inhospitable area of north-west Europe would be nomadic peoples and almost certainly lived entirely by hunting—probably wild boar, bears, wild sheep and cattle, harried by the packs of wolves that roamed the edges of the primeval forests. It took early man several millenia to develop to the relatively advanced stage of being able to clear and cultivate the ground. Archaeologists usually date the period of early settlement with the New Stone Age, or Neolithic period—about 2,400 B.C. It is probable that our earliest tracks and paths—save those made by the earliest hunters—date from this period.

Early man preferred to live in upland areas. Until late medieval times England—even high areas like the Pennines— was largely covered with dense forests, above which only the summits of the hills and high moorlands appeared. Valleys were dense, impenetrable masses of undergrowth and swamp. Chalk and limestone areas must have had great appeal for they had gentle slopes, thin covering of vegetation, flint to use as tools and caves in which to shelter. Barrows and tumuli abound on the higher chalk uplands and, if the many fine stone circles are much to go by, quite a sophisticated civilisation developed. Certainly there was a great deal of movement of people as well as trading, and although by this time geological change had isolated Britain from Continental Europe, implements and weapons were apparently imported. So transport was required by foot and by horses, which were known in Britain in quite early times. The earliest routes along the tops of hills have survived, those on the chalk uplands of the south—the ancient ridgeways as they are known—being quite famous. But Yorkshire has some fine examples.

Certainly the East Riding Wolds provide exactly the kind of low, chalk hills early man chose. There are numerous neolithic long barrows on the Wolds and the North York Moors. Several old tracks along the Wold tops almost connect up lines of tumuli, and it is not fanciful to suggest that they probably date from neolithic times, although many are now buried under the tarmac of a modern minor road. On the North York Moors many of the Riggs have long straight roads over their summits that might well be of very ancient origin. A particularly fine example is the track known as the Hambleton Drove Road which forms a ridgeway along the edge of the Hambleton hills, running from Kilburn, near Thirsk, over the top of Sutton Bank and the north edge of Black Hambleton towards Stokesley.

The next wave of immigrants, known as the "Beaker" people because of their skill in making beaker-shaped pots, also seemed to prefer the lower limestone hills and chalk wolds of East Yorkshire. They were skilled craftsmen and were the first to discover and work Whitby jet. It was these people who built many of the henge monuments of Yorkshire, including the famous Devil's Arrows near Boroughbridge. These are made of Knaresborough gritstone; the transportation of the great hunks of grit over the 6½ miles from Knaresborough must have presented some problems. The descendants of the "Beaker" people, identified by their ability to make urns with rims or "collars," seem to have penetrated further into the Pennines, and remains near Pule Hill at Huddersfield, near Grassington, and near West Tanfield suggest the existence of ancient trans-Pennine trade routes. The road along the south of Rombalds Moor to Baildon was almost certainly an ancient ridgeway before modernisation, as the discovery of late- "Beaker" people ware on Baildon Moor testifies. Many "cup and ring" stones are common on Rombalds and Ilkley Moor— and date from this period about 2,000 B.C. One of the most famous of these remains is the Swastika stone between Addingham and Ilkley on the very crest of Ilkley Moor. It is certain that some kind of track or path must have led past this stone., probably on the line of the modern footpath up from Hebden Gill towards Windgate Nick.

The problem with the Pennines is the fact that tracks across gritstone moors do not survive as certainly and as deeply as those across the soft chalks of the south. The harder rock, and flat tops of bog and peat, do not easily leave traces of man. But it is probable that in Bronze and Iron Age times trade routes existed between the Continent and Ireland using these ancient hill tracks over the Pennines. Many of these have been modernised, but one of the most splendid examples of an ancient ridge track that still survives, much as it must have been in Bronze Age times, is the route known as the High Way which crosses the watershed from the top of Wensleydale into the Eden Valley. It begins at Cotter Bridge on the main Hawes-Sedbergh road about three miles from Hawes and climbs, at first as a fieldpath, up behind the crags of Cotter End. It then follows the ridge round climbing above Lunds and over the head springs of the river Ure, before crossing the infant Eden at Hell Gill and descending down the green shoulder of Mallerstang Edge to join the modern road to Kirkby Stephen near Pendragon Castle.

The High Way thus follows a natural pass through the Pennines, and would be the obvious route to use being well-

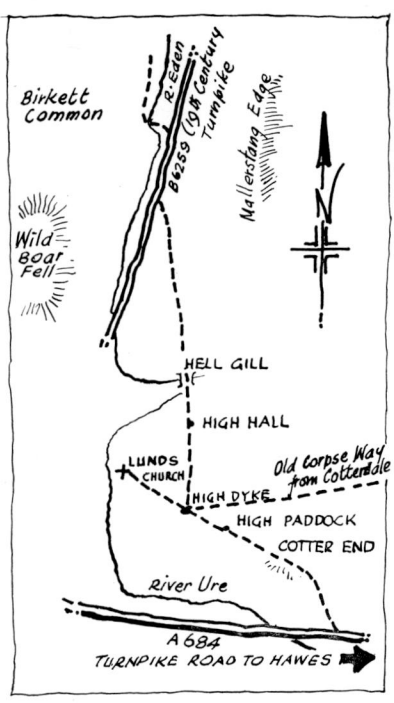

The High Way, a surviving example of a Bronze Age routeway.

drained and free from undergrowth. Pendragon, as the name implies, is of Celtic origin and according to Mallory, King Arthur was the son of Uther of Pendragon. Could this have been the legendary monarch's birth place? Less speculative is the importance of the High Way as a prehistoric and medieval trade route connecting the towns of Ripon and Hawe with Kirkby Stephen and the Scottish Border. In later ages it was an important packhorse route. Several ruined farms still survive up there, including one known as High Paddock which was probably a primitive inn for packhorse men and their beasts. This old route was the main road until the turnpike was built and opened in the 19th century.

The High Way is not so easy to follow now after nearly 150 years of disuse. The start near Cotter Bridge is a faint path up steep pasture. Behind Cotter End it is joined by another old way, the corpse road from Cotterdale along which the parishioners used to carry their dead to Lunds church. Along the ridge top a slight hollow in the ground indicates the way by the wall, and the observant walker will make out tell-tale traces of the old route. Just occasionally vestiges of the stony surface emerge where the way is worn into softer outcrops of limestone. Not far past the fine old Jacobean farm of High Hall the route descends a little to a more modern bridge over Hell Gill—a fissure recently described as one of the wonders of Britain. From here to Mallerstang the way is a broad green swathe, and descending below Mallerstang Edge the greener tinge in the moor grass clearly indicates the outline of this ancient route. It is a fascinating and beautiful walk.

8

2: Roman Roads

I THINK we still have slightly mixed feelings about the Romans–admiration for their incredible efficiency as military conquerors and occupiers mingled with a fear of that very efficiency. It would be wrong to assume that Britain was uncivilised before the Roman Conquest. The region from the Humber to the Tyne was the kingdom of one of the most powerful and civilised Celtic peoples, the Brigantes, who certainly did not welcome or easily capitulate to the southern invaders. Archaeological and documentary evidence suggests that the Roman generals met a fair amount of fierce resistance from the Brigantian chieftains.

It was the greatest of the Roman governors of Britain, Julius Agricola, who finally saw the way to subjugate the Brigantes. The Roman army triumphed largely because of the excellence of its communications, which meant the road system. The legions were highly disciplined and extremely mobile; the success of the Roman military machine depended on the speed with which a general could deploy his relatively small forces in trouble spots. Most of Yorkshire was a trouble spot as the hills, particularly the Pennines, favoured the small bands of tribesmen who retreated to wage guerilla warfare against the imperial power. It was a situation not unlike many in the 20th century.

As military control was not easily achieved, Yorkshire has much more evidence of military occupation than other parts of Roman Britain. The famous Romano-British cities, with their elaborate villas and their public rooms and baths, at Dorchester, Canterbury, Exeter, London, Bath and St. Albans were all in the safe south, while the main settlements of the north, Chester and York, were large and powerful garrison towns. York, in Roman times Eburacum, was developed as a major Roman defence base with the Ninth Legion and later the Sixth being stationed there. It was superbly situated from the Roman point of view, guarding the plain of York and

Left: Roman Way from Bain-bridge to Ribchester near Ribblehead (Bertram Unne). Above: Possible Roman road over Blackstone Edge (W. R. Mitchell.)

served by the river Ouse which ensured plentiful supplies from London and the Continent. It was the road network which largely established York's importance for the London-York highway, known in later ages as the Great North Road or Ermine Street, was the principal route of the times. The Great North Road does not actually go through York, but runs well to the west of the city to Boroughbridge and on to Scotland. If a purely Roman creation it would surely have gone straight to the regional capital, but as it runs direct to the old town of Aldborough or Isurium Brigantum, the capital of the old Brigantian kingdom and still an important settlement in Romano-British times, this suggests that the Romans had taken over an existing ancient highway as their trunk route to the north.

Agricola's other main trunk route in the area was the road from Manchester to Ribchester and Carlisle on the western side of the Pennines. Cross routes between these two main north-south highways divided the Pennines into a series of boxes, guarded by fortresses at frequent intervals. One main route was from Castleford via Slack and Castleshaw to Manchester, while a second important road from Manchester perhaps used the stretch of road over Blackstone Edge before turning north to Ilkley. An important route ran from Tadcaster via Adel and Cookridge over the back of Otley Chevin, close to an old lane still significantly known as York Gate, then to the fort at Ilkley and on via Addingham High Moor to Elslack and Ribchester.

Bainbridge in Wensleydale had strategic significance in Roman times, doubtless guarding the Wensleydale passes including the route over the High Way referred to in the previous chapter. Roads ran over Stake Moss to Buckden and

Ilkley, and over Cam Fell to Ribchester. Both are still unspoiled green lanes over the fells. Further north the pass over Stainmore between Catterick and Carlisle was of enormous importance. In East Yorkshire a road from Lincoln which crossed the Humber at Brough curved towards York with a branch northwards to Malton. Humber Street, a line of Roman road over the Wolds running directly from Brough to Malton, has been traced, and it has been surmised that there must have been several roads eastwards to signal stations on the coast. There is no mistaking the fine old road over Wheeldale moor which led from camps at Cawthorn towards Whitby

There were two main kinds of Roman road, the Campaigning or Pioneer roads and the Viae Publicae. Pioneer roads, as the name implies, were hurriedly-made affairs of logs designed to give assistance to invading armies and to maintain rough and ready supply lines. Viae Publicae were much more carefully constructed. They were between 16 and 24 feet wide, allowing troops to march six abreast, and were often smoothly

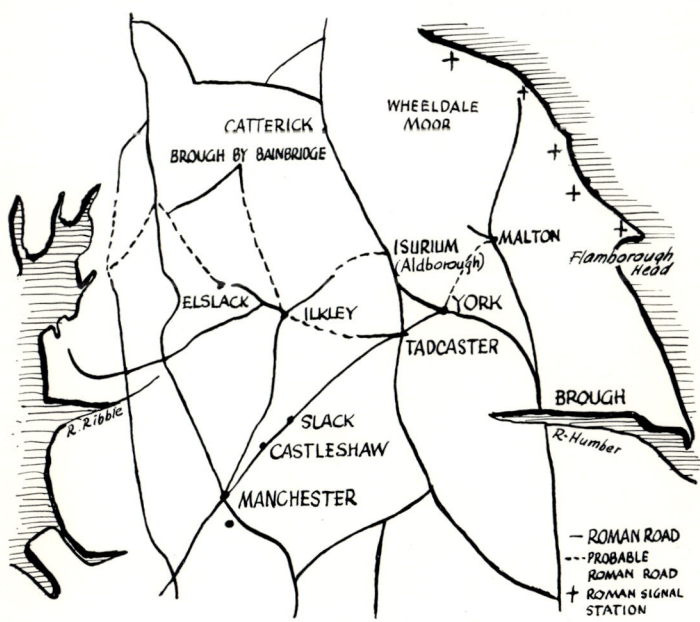

Sketch of the Roman roads in the North.

paved to allow chariots to use them. The secret of Roman road-building was good foundations—layers of beaten earth, stones, filling, cement and flagstones to make a hard and firm surface. The completed road was sometimes raised several feet from the ground, thus providing a perfectly drained causeway giving excellent views of the surrounding country-side. Contrary to popular opinion, Roman road-makers had the wit to divert from a straight line when faced with a difficult natural hazard.

The roads were built by the legions as military undertakings, but were maintained by the State if important enough (Imperial roads) or local authorities if less important. Posthouses were set up a day's riding distance apart, supplied with accommodation, horses, light carriages and postillions, and important people and messages could be carried at great speed. There was also a great deal of non-military traffic—chariots, foot travellers, lumbering four-wheel tradesmen's wagons and horsemen. Britain had a transport system on a national scale, the like of which was not seen again until at least the end of the 18th century. So excellent were the roads that many of them have never gone out of use, and our present road system is still dependent on what were once Roman roads. The story of the Great North Road is the history of Britain itself. It still dominates Yorkshire, almost dividing East and West Ridings. If only the traffic could be stopped for a year or two to enable archaeologists to uncover its buried treasures!

There are quite a few strips of Roman road that have not been buried under tarmac or turned over by the plough. Some odd strips of Roman ridge can still be found alongside the Great North Road or the Tadcaster-York highway, although in recent years damaged by ploughing. There are the two campaigning roads from Bainbridge, cutting across the fells like ruled lines, and there is a half-buried stretch of the Ilkley-Aldborough road on Blubberhouses Moor. The most celebrated example in Yorkshire is surely that magnificent stretch known as Wade's Causeway after a mythical North Yorkshire giant, which curves over Wheeldale Moor near Goathland. Preserved on the sandy moor, and now protected by the Ministry of Works, the road retains even its original camber. The surface stones are broken and weathered, but the broad and bold curve of the road across the heather is an oddly stirring sight.

3: Anglian Footpaths

ALTHOUGH the Romans managed to spread their highly sophisticated Mediterranean culture even among the hostile Brigantes, it was an uneasy and eventful occupation in Yorkshire. There were constant threats of attack from fresh invaders along the vulnerable east coast, and a chain of signal fortresses was constructed on the cliffs at Filey, Scarborough, Ravenscar, Kettleness, Saltburn and other places to warn the colony of invading warships. Once the protective shield of the legions departed in the 5th century, it was inevitable that these invaders would quickly overrun the country. When they came they found relatively little resistance, and burned, pillaged and looted, sending the Britons to seek the refuge of the hills. What did the uncouth Angles make of the fine architecture of places like York? One can imagine their bewilderment at the sheer massiveness and beauty of the Roman buildings as opposed to their own rough dwelling houses. As an old Anglo-Saxon poem "The Ruin" expressed it:

Snapped rooftrees, towers fallen,
the work of the Giants, the stonesmiths,
mouldereth.

And what did they make of the great roads, the "straetes" as they called them in their crude tongue? They built their houses close to the roads, inhabited the shells of the cities and fortresses they had ransacked, and divided their lands by the roads. Parish boundaries, even today, are frequently divided by the line of a Roman road.

Ethelfrith, King of Deira, drove the Celts in the 6th century north to Cumbria beyond the Ribble, and westwards over the Dee. But the powerful kingdom of Deira (modern Yorkshire) was held at bay by the Mercians in the south, and between them was the old Celtic kingdom of Elmet acting as a sort of buffer state between the rival powers. It was in Elmet in 655

13

A.D. that the aged Mercian King Penda was defeated by the Christian King Oswy at the battle of Whinmoor; it is said that in gratitude for the victory Oswy gave the lands at Whitby on which the abbey was built. No sooner were the Anglian kingdoms at peace with one another than new invaders from east and west, Dane and Norseman, were asserting their claim to the territory.

The Anglo-Saxons were an agrarian people. There was relatively little trade on a national scale, and what there was continued to be served by the surviving Roman highways. As the names "ley" and "thwaite" imply, early settlements were literally clearings in the primeval forest which covered so much of Britain; they were generally in fertile lowlands rather than on the bleak moorlands. Villages and hamlets developed haphazardly, and between villages and farmsteads beaten earthpaths walked by man and beast appeared. Areas would be organised first of all into tribal units and then later by the more sophisticated principle of "wapentakes" when local warriors met at alloted intervals, making their way to the "Skyrack" or Shire Oak to give their allegiance to their leader or earl, and through him to their king. Many of these paths, bending round every field and cottage, have developed into the intricate web of modern minor roads, often narrow and hidden behind tall hedgerows. There are plenty of these all over Yorkshire, but particularly in the rich and well-settled areas of the North and East Ridings.

Others have remained as field paths between what were strip fields, or perhaps over areas of common land. When many of these fields and commons were enclosed in the 18th century the paths remained in use, and stiles— from Anglo-Saxon "stigh" meaning a narrow way—were built through or over walls to keep the way open. Many of the paths were "parishioners" ways leading to and from church.

Nearly all journeys in Saxon times were on foot. There was some wheeled traffic, ox-drawn drays or wains, and a few nobles possessed horses, but the vast majority walked. Many lanes and village field paths have therefore been in constant use for a thousand years. The hamlet of Stainburn near Harrogate, for instance, has a church of Norman origin, and it is possible that an earlier building—perhaps of wood—stood on the site. It is safe to assume that the network of old lanes and paths, only one or two of which are open for motor traffic, have been in use since the church was built, and particularly so the little path still used by worshippers which leads from the hamlet to the church. There might have been a period when they were disused—for example when William the Conqueror carried out his brutal harrying of the north which meant butchering every man, woman and child in sight and razing every building to the ground, and during the 14th century "Black Death." But otherwise these paths across field and meadow were constantly used by the farm labourer going to work or to church, by his family, by the priest, by tinkers, by tradesmen. A thousand years of history is written into humble little footpaths.

Only in the 20th century has their existence been threatened. There has been a steady but constant depopulation of the remoter areas which has accelerated in recent years, and also a growth of motor transport. Once a farm labourer would think nothing of a two or more mile walk to the village; he now uses a van or tractor. Villagers own cars. Even a schoolboy will wait for the school bus rather than walk home, but then often the village school is closed and he must travel to the big comprehensive school in the nearby town. For the first time since the Black Death it seems as if the paths are to remain overgrown, the stiles to rot away, Farmers and landowners are often anxious to see the end of a path. Increased ploughing of pastures has made paths a nuisance, and the fact that they are a right of way matters less than the cost of keeping a stile in repair or having by law to keep a bull away from a path. Many landowners have supported recent moves to bring about the rationalisation of old paths, which is a polite way of referring to their elimination on a massive scale. The law relating to the existence of a right of way refers to its usage over the last 20 or 30 years, not to its usage in the 13th century, and many fine old footpaths have been lost because local people

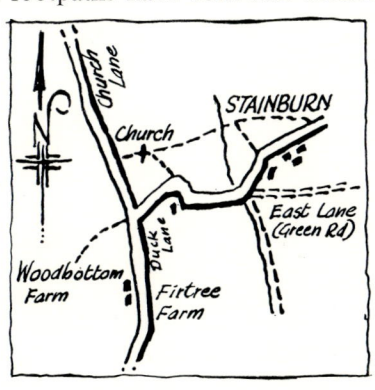

parishioners' ways: Stainburn near Harrogate.

15

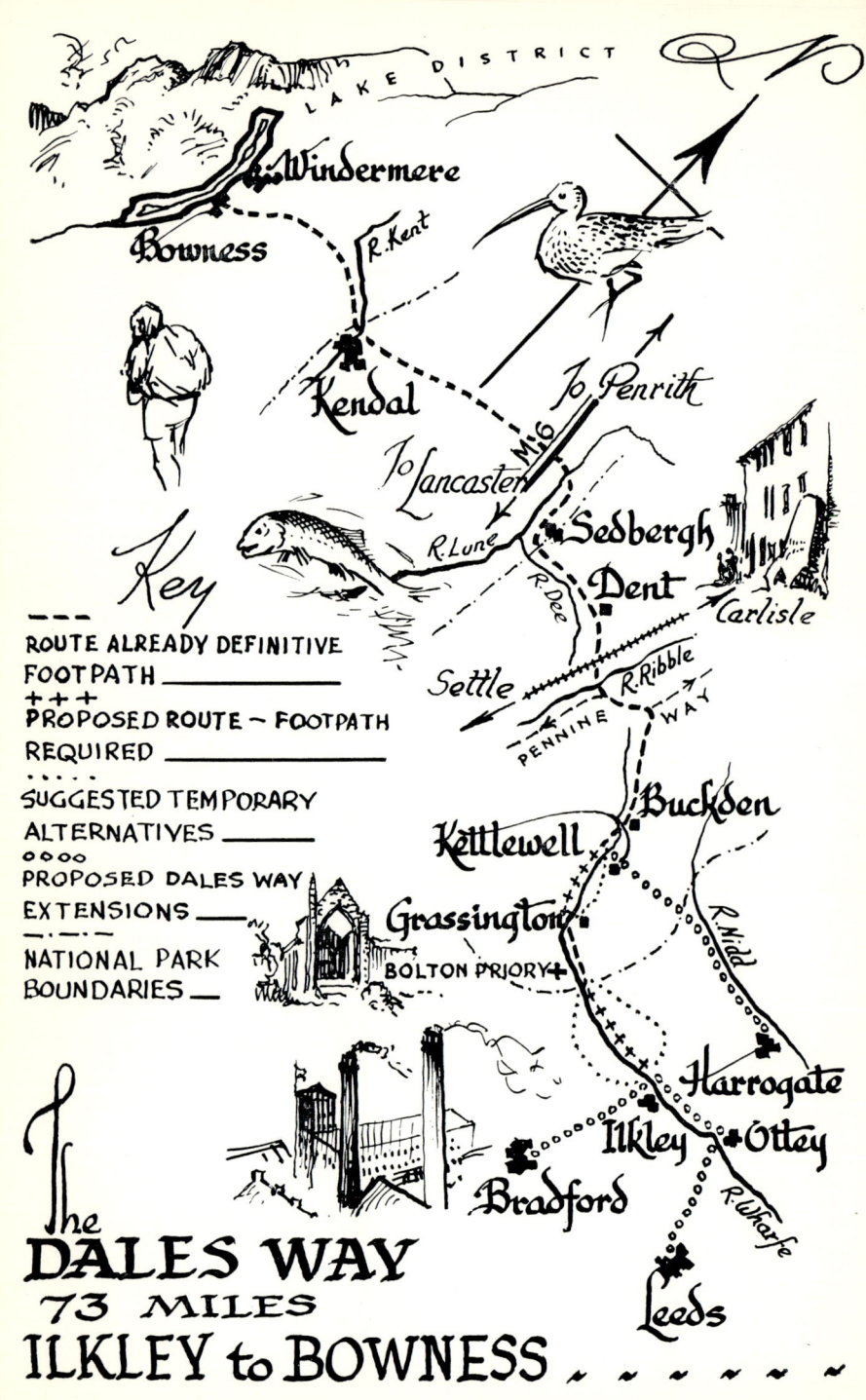

LAKE DISTRICT

Windermere

Bowness

R. Kent

Kendal

To Lancaster

To Penrith

M.6

R. Lune

R. Dee

Sedbergh

Dent

Carlisle

Settle

R. Ribble

PENNINE WAY

Key

— — —
ROUTE ALREADY DEFINITIVE
FOOTPATH ——————————
+++
PROPOSED ROUTE ~ FOOTPATH
REQUIRED ——————————
· · · ·
SUGGESTED TEMPORARY
ALTERNATIVES ——————
∘∘∘∘
PROPOSED DALES WAY
EXTENSIONS ——————
— · — · —
NATIONAL PARK
BOUNDARIES ——

Buckden

Kettlewell

Grassington

BOLTON PRIORY

R. Nidd

Harrogate

Ilkley

Otley

Bradford

R. Wharfe

Leeds

The
DALES WAY
73 MILES
ILKLEY to BOWNESS

were not willing to give evidence—perhaps against their own landlords—of using the path in the last few years.

The motor car age has another side to it. Increasingly people are coming out into the countryside for a day or a longer stay. The crowded roads no longer make motoring the pleasure it was a few years ago, and people are now realising that the old paths provide a remarkably fresh and pleasant way of seeing the countryside. There is also quite a fashion for purchasing a cottage in the country for weekend use, or retiring there. Active middle-aged people are eager to explore the local walks and village people, increasingly disturbed at the loss of their old paths, are urging local parish councils to preserve these ancient ways. National bodies—such as the Ramblers' Association and the Commons Society—representing townspeople and country lovers, have been working extremely actively over recent years to collect evidence to prove the existence of rights of way.

The 1949 National Parks Act gave National Park authorities powers to create new long-distance footpaths. The most famous of these, the Pennine Way running from Derbyshire to the Scottish Border, is extremely popular. East Riding Ramblers are negotiating for a splendid footpath in an area short of paths, a Wolds Way through some of the finest countryside of the Yorkshire Wolds between North Ferriby and Filey Brigg. The Cleveland Way, between Helmsley and the North York Moors coastline, was opened in 1969, and West Riding Ramblers are hoping to create the Dales Way, a 73-mile river-side footpath from Ilkley to Bowness using old rights of way for much of its route. The Lyke Wake Walk is now a broad and beautiful track over the North York Moors, and no one dare argue about rights of way along it!

This all goes to prove that footpaths are no historical anachronism. They are a part of our heritage, suddenly important again, and they have an individuality, beauty and sense of timelessness that is precious in a highly industrialised age. To follow a winding way, to feel the very contours of the land beneath your feet, to be so close to the sights, smell and even touch of the countryside, is to re-establish contact with a world we have almost forgotten. Once footpaths were necessary for labour. Now they are necessary for recreation—in the fullest sense of the word.

Opposite: The Dales Way typifies the kind of long-distance footpaths which are being established under the 1949 National Parks Act.

4: Medieval Highways

WE tend to think of the Normans as men who imposed a feudal order on primitive, chaotic Saxon society. This is a long way from the truth, for England under the later Saxon kings was a well-organised and civilised society, something that contrasted sharply with the dictatorship of William's rule of armed might. Certainly if art and literature are anything to go by, the Norman Conquest was a plunging of England back into the Dark Ages. Following a rising by the English at York in 1070, William put the entire county to waste with the sole exception of the property of his favourite Ilbert de Lacy, whose chief stronghold at Pontefract was developed so as to be centrally placed for overseeing the de Lacy domain. The de Lacys also constructed a powerful fortress at Clitheroe to control the unfortunate inhabitants in the west, while to the south of the county the Earls de la Warenne made Wakefield their administrative centre with fortified keeps at Conisborough and Sandal to ensure subjugation of their tenants.

The feudal barons sub-let their vast estates to suitable tenants, the Lords of the Manor, who were responsible for administrating their own properties. The feudal system required a fair amount of travelling on a regional scale, both within the smaller unit of the manor and the larger unit of the baronial region. It is probable that many of our existing roads began as manorial ways between the larger regional Honours and the manors. It is not without significance that Wakefield has become the county town of the West Riding, and the patterns of roads from Wakefield, Pontefract, Richmond and Skipton still reflect their old importance. It is probable for example that the road between Pontefract and Clitheroe, via Bradford, Haworth and Colne, would be a very important highway in feudal times, the landlords along the route being required to provide men to safeguard the lord and his retinue when they travelled that way. Officially, manors were responsible for maintaining the roads that passed through them, but it seems to have been a very haphazard affair. There was probably little road building as such, it being more a question of throwing down earth and stones when the mire got too deep and occasionally repairing a bridge.

The feudal lords also established forests for hunting. A medieval forest was not quite the same thing as a modern forest; it was really a stretch of open land reserved for a lord's hunts, development being controlled and poaching strictly forbidden. The forests were administered by keepers in lodges —famous examples of forest lodges are Barden Tower which controlled the Clifford lands in Wharfedale and Gaunt's Castle, Haveragh in the Forest of Knaresborough, and it is probable that many of the roads through mid-Wharfedale and Nidderdale originated as forest tracks. Even more important than these were the roads leading to the many country fairs. The right to hold a fair could only be given by royal authority, and many famous Yorkshire market towns, such as Otley, Knaresborough, Boroughbridge, Grassington, Ripon and Pateley Bridge, received their charters to hold fairs in the 13th and 14th centuries. Market fairs were essential to the economy of feudal Yorkshire, and around the town or village regular traffic developed the roads into something approaching the pattern we know today. Dr. Raistrick, in *Green Tracks on the Pennines,* has noted how the small village of Kirkby Malzeard had far greater importance than it has today because of its fair, and this is reflected in the road pattern. Many other small villages, for instance Hampsthwaite and Ripley in Nidderdale, once held regular fairs.

Nothing boosted medieval trade more than the growth of the monasteries. When the Archbishop of York gave land in 1132 in an obscure little valley of the river Skell, did he suspect that he was helping to establish one of the most powerful Cistercian monasteries in all Europe, and creating the basis of Yorkshire's woollen industry? Fountains Abbey was immensely wealthy. It owed its power partially to the skill and industry of its brethren and partly to the fact that devout and hell-fearing landowners, afraid for their immortal souls and regretting a worldy life, frequently gave lands to the abbey to offset the obvious risks. The monks used their gifts well; they had many thousands of acres in the Craven area alone, besides extensive estates in Calderdale, Wharfedale and Nidderdale. Byland Abbey had lands in Nidderdale; Furness in upper Ribblesdale; Bolton in Wharfedale and Malhamdale; while Sawley had estates in Bowland and around Gargrave.

It was impossible for monks to manage their vast and scattered estates from one central point, so a system of granges was established. A small group of brothers would manage the estates from the granges which would need an efficient system of communication with the parent body. The simplest way of doing this was by long trains of pack-ponies, admirably suited to the hilly terrain of the Dales. These tough and sturdy little beasts were in great demand for this kind of work, and remained in service in the hillier regions of Yorkshire almost until the 19th century. German hunting ponies, called Jaeger ponies or jaggers, were preferred but sometimes Galloway ponies were used. They were able to carry up to about $2\frac{1}{2}$ cwt, and conveyed their burdens either in packs fastened to a wooden saddle designed to spread the load (a surviving pack-horse saddle of the 18th century is to be found in the Yorkshire Folk Museum, Shibden Hall, Halifax) or in tough pannier baskets. Ponies could climb the steepest hillside and tread across the stoniest path with ease.

The monks mined coal and lead, cut peat, prepared charcoal and grew wheat, but their most important contribution of all was wool. They reared sheep with great skill; the monks of Fountains fattened their herds on the rich pastures of Borrowdale in the Lake District, and then brought them back to Yorkshire for shearing and wintering. Kilnsey in Wharfedale was the regular shearing place; the old monastic drove road, Mastiles Lane, still survives with the remains of crosses that once marked the route, a very common practice from medieval times onwards.

Until the time of Edward III most of Yorkshire's wool was exported to Flanders to be processed overseas, and the monks transported their produce on horseback to convenient ports for shipment. The towns of Yarm, Beverley, Knottingley and Boroughbridge had considerable importance in medieval times as being the limit of the navigable sections of their respective rivers, boats being much cheaper and efficient than

Left: Mastiles Lane (Bertram Unne).

horses. York, capable of berthing larger vessels on the Ouse, was soon to establish itself as the principal trading and export centre of medieval Yorkshire. Wool was England's first major export industry, and the woolsack remains a symbol of our national wealth and independence. Many present-day roads first began their existence as monastic tracks used by pack-ponies. The road from Ramsgill via Bouthwaite (once a grange) over Fountains Earth Moor to Fountains Abbey and the road between Pateley Bridge and Middlesmoor were both originally monastic ways.

The hills of Yorkshire, which for centuries made transport and communication difficult for the inhabitants, have pre-served many of the old tracks and paths used by monastic packhorses, and although they remained in use for so long they retain their medieval character. There is the fine old pack-horse way, almost certainly monastic in origin, over Horsehead Moor climbing up from Yockenthwaite in Langstrothdale to Littondale, and the superb little track—walled on either side—that goes from Austwick to Feizor. From Feizor—where there was once a grange—the way can still be followed, a worn hollow in the soft limestone climbing dramatically by Smear-sett Scar before descending to the famous pack-horse bridge over the Ribble at Stainforth. From here the way perhaps continued by Goat Lane and Silverdale to Halton Gill and over Horsehead Moor (possibly part of the Lancaster-Richmond route) or else due east via Malham and Mastiles Lane for Pateley Bridge, Ripon and York.

Long after the dissolution of the monasteries, pack-horses continued to serve the needs of Dales industries and agriculture. By the 17th century enormous numbers of horses must have been crossing and re-crossing the Dales under the eyes of watchful packhorsemen. The average number of horses in a train was about 20, the leading horse being known as the bell horse, and according to many contemporary accounts the tinkle of bells across the fellsides was a familiar sound.

Although pack-horses could with great ease manage stone tracks that would wreck wheeled vehicles, they could be bogged down in marsh or peat. Causeways, long lines of smooth flagstones winding up a lonely fellside or across a wild moorland, were often laid for them in such places, and there are still many of them to be found all over the Pennines, Splendid examples are to be seen between Leeds and Bradford. and in the upper Calder valley around Todmorden and Hebden Bridge. A well-known and popular paved way goes from

Left: Thorns Gill bridge (Cyril Harrington).

Dick Hudson's, Eldwick, over towards Ilkley Moor, and there is another fine example on Middleton Moor above Ilkley. One that is almost certainly a monastic causeway is Monks Trod between Grosmont Priory and Whitby Abbey. The paving stones can be followed almost to the bottom of the 199 steps although they are not always visible—sometimes the way is a tree-shaded lane, sometimes it is buried underneath a tarmac road, and by Ruswarp it seems to have vanished altogether. Then just a short way before Whitby it emerges as a lovely field path making an attractive short cut to the town centre.

Horses can manage shallow fords easily enough, but when a river rises after winter rains they can be rather difficult. In many places fine stone pack-horse bridges, just wide enough to allow a line of ponies to cross and with low parapets to prevent a load being hindered, were built. They show Dales architecture at its very best—several famous examples have survived in the Pennines some, like Stainforth, being preserved as monuments. The pack-horse bridge over the Washburn at Dob Park is well known, while equally fine is New Bridge over the Nidd near Hampsthwaite. My favourite pack-horse bridge, on the Craven Way between Ribblesdale and Dentdale at Thorns Gill, is in very serious danger of being lost. The gill is a narrow, turbulent ravine, and the bridge—a single frail arch—is supported quite delicately between the two edges. It has lost its parapet, but its perfect simple design and structure keep it secure even though any mortar seems to have long since eroded away. But it will not last for ever; already a large side fragment of the slender arch has fallen away, and unless it is repaired it will inevitably soon collapse. Unfortun-

22

ately no-one will take responsibility for the bridge. Although it is an ancient right of way modern usage cannot be proved, and neither landowner nor county council seem prepared to take any action. Its loss would be a tragedy—Thorns Gill bridge is a gem.

Pack-horse transport was a thriving industry by the late middle ages. Men and their beasts needed rest, shelter and food at frequent intervals, and along the old pack-horse routes inns came into being. Many of these have vanished or been demolished, but one or two (those along modernised roads) have survived and become modern taverns. Tan Hill, England's highest inn with its old coal mine, came into being in this way. A famous packman's house was the inn at Gearstones, near Ribblehead, which was at the junction of several ways. The building is still there, but it is no longer an inn.

It is still possible to follow at least one pack-horse route across the Pennines which is much as it was in the 17th century. This is the route known as Rapes Highway, Pace Gate (gate being an old dialect word for road) or the Marsden Packhorse Road. It begins in Lancashire at Milnrow, almost certainly leaving the main Rochdale road at Charles Lane. Significantly the old highway crosses under the new Trans-Pennine motorway before climbing the moorland. At one point remnants of old pounds, probably used for ponies, can be seen, while further on the foundations of cottages perhaps indicate the site of a hostelry and paddock. The track passes Piethorn reservoir, reaching the main A672 behind the *Ram's Head Inn,* and continues in almost the same direction under the shoulder of Great Hill before coming to the A640. A fine old guide stoop still faintly inscribed with the name Pace Gate indicates the way from here, a faint green track over the moors marked by fallen granite posts carved with the words "P.H. Road." These are the result of a successful law suit fought in 1908 by Marsden Council, which was determined to make sure there would be no mistakes in the future. Most of the posts are now fallen. The track emerges at Eastergate pack-horse bridge where there used to be the *Packhorse Inn,* kept by a woman called Esther Schofield, hence the name Easter-gate. A few years ago a storm damaged the bridge and the causeway which leads into Marsden, but the damage has now been repaired. Rapes Highway is a fine 11-mile walk, and well worth the effort. It was in regular use until about the 1820s.

It seems likely that this and other routes across the Pennines were used by the "broggers" taking wool to and from small

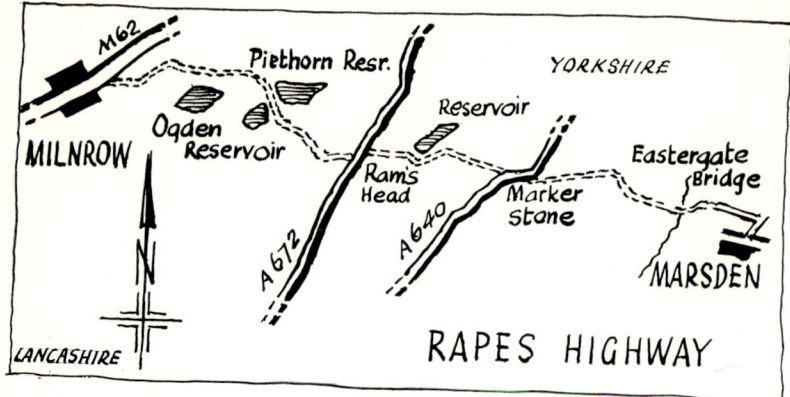

An old pack-horse route which can still be followed across the Pennines is the Rapes Highway running from Milnrow in Lancashire to Marsden in Yorkshire.

manufacturers on each side of the Pennines, especially important when weaving was still a cottage industry. The "Roman" road over Blackstone Edge, which some experts now dispute as to its completely Roman origin, was extremely important and busy with Rochdale-Halifax traffic in the 17th century, and is the route described so vividly by Daniel Defoe in the Yorkshire section of his *Tour through England and Wales*. Other familiar travellers on the 17th century highways were "badgers," a combination of the tinker and the travelling shopkeeper, carrying their goods on a couple of ponies, visiting outlying farms to provide urgently needed goods and doing a certain amount of exchange and barter. So familiar were these callers that their regular track over the moors became associated with them, and was sometimes known as Badger Gate. One such example runs from Beamsley over Blubberhouses Moor to Timble; the route is still there, and even has a guide stoop above Middleton giving distances in "customary" miles to "Skipton, Rippon, Otley and Ilkleaa."

Dr. Raistrick in his *Green Tracks on the Pennines* has written at length on the mass of pack-horse ways in the region. One particularly important group of regular travellers were the salters—the men carrying the salt from the Cheshire mines to the towns of Yorkshire and north-east England where it was in great demand for preserving meat. Dr. Raistrick traces the probable route from Lancashire, as evidenced by the place names, from Salterforth through the Aire Gap and along the present Skipton-Harrogate road bearing north by Salterhill near Harrogate along what is still called Psalter Lane.

Drovers required a different kind of route from pack-horse men—a herd of sheep or cattle is best driven down a broad lane where there are preferably not too many other travellers to break up or disturb the herd. There was enormous traffic, right up to the building of the railways, in cattle from Scotland which were driven on their own feet from the Highlands to be fattened on the rich pastures of Craven before being sold in the markets of Skipton. Most livestock was transported on its own feet—cattle, horses, sheep and goats. Even a gaggle of geese was not an uncommon sight; for a long journey the practice was to dip their feet in tar and then in sand to give them a hard sole. A drover's life must have been a hard one, walking a dozen or so miles a day, sleeping rough and hoping that sickness or tiredness did not destroy the beasts before they could be safely delivered. They preferred to take their herd over the quiet, lonely hilltops, along the broad tracks that still survive. There are several old drover's roads in the Dales— notably Mastiles Lane and the broad track over the head of Dentdale and Widdale Fell still known as the "driving" road.

Of lugubrious interest were the corpse ways, one or two of which are still to be found in the Dales. It was often necessary to carry a corpse some distance to the nearest piece of con- secrated ground, and if the settlement was large enough the accustomed route soon became known as the corpse way. The most famous example is between Keld and Grinton in Swale- dale, where thoughtful people even constructed ledges on which a body could be rested on its last journey. As poor hill-farmers could not always afford a coffin these ledges must have been appreciated in warm weather. If the words of the splendid Lyke Wake Dirge are to be believed there must be one or two other corpse ways on the North York Moors.

Apart from foot travellers and pack-horses, there was a certain amount of wheeled traffic where the conditions of the roads allowed it. But the sprung coach was not invented until the reign of Elizabeth, and as riding in an unsprung wagon over a rocky road could have a permanently damaging effect on one's bone structure, most people travelled, like Chaucer's pilgrims, on horseback. When one reflects that the estimated population of Yorkshire in the Domesday Survey was a mere 8,000, and even by 1379 it was only 90,000, travel on medieval Yorkshire roads must have been a lonely experience. It was certainly dangerous with robbers and brigands round every corner, and travellers usually went together whenever possible.

5: Turnpike Roads

WHEELED traffic, mostly wagons and carts, was increasing steadily on the roads during the 15th and 16th centuries. The Highways Act of 1555 attempted to improve the appalling state of the roads by ordering parishes and not landowners to be responsible for the repair of roads. Every parishioner had to work for four days of the year on the parish roads, though of course the wealthy could pay others to do the work for them. In 1563 this was increased to six days, but apart from the occasional scouring out of ditches the work does not seem to have been done with much zeal or efficiency. The only actual construction work seems to have been the making of pack-horse causeways by the side of miry lanes. Several of these raised ways have survived in Yorkshire, particularly in the Leeds and Bradford area, and the Long Causeway in Adel is just such a way. It is not without significance that Yorkshire folk to this day refer to what the rest of England call a pavement as a "causey."

In order for some reasonable system of communications to exist throughout the nation, the government had by the 16th century set up a fairly comprehensive postal service between the major towns. This was run by a series of postmasters who each kept a stable of good horses and provided accommodation. Important government dispatches, and later private mail, could be sent by means of the postboys who rode at speed between the posthouses. The postmaster would deliver letters in his own locality and collect letters to be delivered elsewhere, and the system was also used by important government officials who would find fresh horses awaiting them at each posting inn. Unfortunately so many people began to abuse the system, and so many "important" government messengers began to travel, that the service was soon in danger of breaking down. The exchequer therefore decided to benefit from the abuse, and made posthorses available to all for a sum. Journeys along the posting routes cost threepence per mile (paid in advance), but a guide was also necessary—probably more for the safety of the horses than that of the travellers—and he had to be paid handsomely. If the horse was injured, imprisonment could follow so it could be a very expensive business. Average speeds, officially, were 7 m.p.h. in summer and 6 m.p.h. in winter, and the maximum luggage was 30 lbs.

It was expensive, but at least it was a relatively rapid service. Up to about 60 miles a day could be managed, and services were operated through Yorkshire along the Great North Road and from Liverpool through Rochdale and Halifax to Bradford and Leeds. A cheaper way of making a journey between two towns, if sufficient capital was available, was to buy a horse, ride it to the destination and then with skilful salesmanship sell it at that town for as much as the purchase price if not slightly more. Again this could be disastrous if the animal was injured on the journey. But even as late as the 18th century most people simply walked; it will be remembered how Jeannie Deans in Scott's *Heart of Midlothian* walked from Edinburgh to London to see the queen, or how old Mr. Earnshaw in *Wuthering Heights* made the journey on foot from the Haworth moors to Liverpool to bring back the waif Heathcliffe. The wealthy could avoid walking, even through the streets of a town, by hiring a sedan chair. These were at the height of their popularity in the 16th and 17th centuries, and gentry sometimes had themselves carried to destinations well outside the town. Few people, though, could have emulated the French lady who in 1603 had herself carried from Edinburgh to London along the Great North Road by a team of eight suffering chairmen.

Coaches were being developed, the first one being seen in London in 1556. The difference between a coach and a wagon is in the springs; instead of feeling every stone in the road, passengers in a coach are suspended between springs which absorb the shocks and give a much more comfortable and smooth ride. By the early 17th century traffic jams were already common in London, and the diarist John Aubrey was deploring the effeminacy of young men who travelled in coaches instead of riding, like true men should, on horseback. Coaches were all very well on the cobbled streets of a town, but people insisted on using them on the wretched country roads which were still little more than beaten earth tracks, passable perhaps in dry summer weather but in rain or winter thick seas of mud. The habit of avoiding the worst mud in the centre of the roads caused them to broaden out until they were enormous belts of impenetrable quagmire. By the side of modern roads one can sometimes see broad grassy strips, occasionally enclosed into narrow fields, which were created in the pre-turnpike era. A good example is on the Leeds-Otley

Pre-turnpike travel exemplified by the broad muddy road with wagons sinking into the mire, and the preponderance of foot travel. The engraving depicts the road leading from Beacon Hill towards the Humber estuary (collection of J. D. McDonald).

old road along the top of The Chevin.

It is difficult for us to imagine just how vile roads were in the 17th and 18th centuries. One William Kemp, travelling through Yorkshire in 1600, reported: "At length coming to a splash of water and mud which could not be avoided I fetched a rise, yet fell in over the ankles at the farther end. My youth that followed me took his jump and stuck in the middle." Another traveller in 1654 wrote that "the highway leading from Leeds to Wakebridge and so to Seacroft and so to Kiddal toward Yorke hath been in so great a decay that travellers can hardly pass." The Leeds historian, Ralph Thoresby, reported that the "waters" on the roads about Leeds were "very deep" in 1680, while Walpole wrote in 1708 that "the way was very deep and in so many places so dangerous for the coach that we walked on foot," and commented that there were "very black" roads about Leeds. In 1712, travelling between Leeds and Harewood, he reported that "some part of the way is as rocky as can well be supposed on the most remote parts of the island," but perhaps his crowning experience was travelling into Sheffield where his coach fell into a "big black ditch" requiring extra horses to haul it out. In the early 18th century the fastest coaches sometimes managed to reach London in one piece from Yorkshire in four days, but in winter the journey took at least a week.

In a nation where trade was expanding rapidly during the great period of peace and prosperity of the late 17th and early 18th centuries the roads clearly had to be improved. They were stifling development. Dr. Raistrick has observed how the foddering of ponies in the Grassington area to serve the needs of the growing lead-mine industry was reaching saturation point. Heavy wagons and lumbering, ill-sprung coaches were tearing the road surfaces to ribbons. Something had to be done, and it was. Following an Act of Parliament in 1663, the first turnpike trust was established on the Great North Road. These trusts were a simple but effective method of raising money to finance the building and repair of roads; a group of trustees, usually landowners and merchants who had vested interests in seeing improvement in roads, financed the remaking of the stretch of road in question and sealed the road by spiked turnpike barriers which were only opened to travellers on payment of a toll. Keepers were employed at the toll-booths, either by paying them a salary or by allowing them to pay a fixed sum to the trustees and make a living out of the tolls. At the first toll-gate the charges were: Wagon 1s, coach 6d, cart 8d, horse 1d, 20 sheep or lambs 1s. 2d, oxen 5d, hogs 2d. Tolls were largely assessed by the amount of potential damage the vehicles or animals might do to the repaired surface, coaches being less damaging than heavy wagons.

The outcry against the tolls was enormous. What had been a free right of way from earliest times was now suddenly obstructed, and there were riots and angry scenes everywhere. But with traffic increasing and road conditions worsening they had to come and merchants and landowners had their say over the wishes of outraged local populations, although not without an intense struggle. There were riots all over the North, perhaps the most violent of all being in Yorkshire. The town crier in Selby in the 1740s encouraged the mob to take axes and chop up the new turnpikes. Riots preceeded the turnpikes in Wharfedale and around the Harrogate area, and when the Keighley-Wakefield turnpike was established in 1753 an angry mob met at the *Brown Cow,* Bingley, with a view to smashing the barriers. Perhaps the most violent occurrences of all were around Leeds; in the same year, 1753, a carter was arrested for refusing to pay the toll at the Beeston turnpike, and in the ensuing brawl eight people were killed.

With the demand for new roads came new techniques to build them. Coaches required smooth, hard surfaces, and it was the work of a great Yorkshire engineer which supplied the essential breakthrough in 18th century highway engineering. In many ways Jack Metcalf was one of the most extraordinary and brilliant men of his time, and it is an odd quirk of fate that someone like Stephenson could have become a national hero while Metcalf, who overcame a devastating handicap to achieve parallel feats of engineering skill, should have remained in relative obscurity. Metcalf was a man of incredible energy. Born in 1717 at Knaresborough, he was blinded by smallpox at six. In spite of this he was a lively boy, an expert climber, fiddler and swimmer who often rescued people from the dangerous river Nidd. He somehow managed to be a skilled horseman and often guided travellers in the area. On one particularly adventurous trip he rode from Knaresborough to Whitby, from there taking a boat to London. He obviously benefited from his experience because the enterprising young man was soon operating a carting service between the newly established spa of Harrogate and the sea, aimed at bringing fresh fish inland. He also operated a stage-wagon service between York and Knaresborough.

His career was interrupted by the 1745 rebellion, and he joined General Wade to defeat the Highlanders at Culloden. He seems to have profited in two ways from his visit, both in bringing back Scottish stockings and ponies to increase his commercial activities, and in learning about General Wade's road-building exploits in the Highlands. It was as a carter, though, that his interest in roads developed. The highway between Boroughbridge and Knaresborough, was in a wretched state at Minskip and Ferrensby, and Metcalf repaired the surface so well that he was offered the contract for the road between Harrogate and Knaresborough which was ferociously boggy. It had defied many previous attempts at repair and was the despair of local worthies. To everyone's astonishment and probable ridicule, Metcalf had a simple but dramatically effective solution. He covered the bog with masses and masses of tied bundles of heather and "floated" the hard surface of the road over these bundles. The road was superb; hard, firm and dry.

Contract after contract followed, and Metcalf was soon the leading road engineer of the North. Many turnpikes over difficult and boggy land were constructed by him; there was the Harrogate-Harewood road, the Leeds-Harewood, the Leeds-Chapeltown, the Broughton-Addingham, the Millbridge -Halifax, the Wakefield-Denby, the Huddersfield-Halifax, the Grassington-Pateley Bridge, as well as many others in Yorkshire, Derbyshire and Lancashire. His methods were unorthodox; he first surveyed the ground himself, feeling the way with his staff and testing the surface and gradients before deciding on the route and the location of culverts, embankments and earthworks. His secret—like the Romans—was to give his roads really firm and hard foundations. Perhaps his

Right: Pre-turnpike milestone near Draughton, Skipton (Colin Speakman). Far right: Turnpike milestone at Thirsk (C. D. Gibbons).

most brilliant achievement was his work in 1759 on the Wakefield-Austerlands turnpike, which is the Huddersfield-Manchester road over Standedge. Faced with the impassable bog on Pule Hill, he again "floated" the road on bundles of heather and provided a finely engineered highway that did much to encourage trade between Lancashire and Yorkshire. Though the road was subsequently rebuilt to give even easier gradients, much of the route is as Metcalf surveyed it. His achievement has been given fresh light by the recent work on the Lancashire-Yorkshire motorway, which for all the sophisticated engineering aids is proving a formidable task. Metcalf worked with his staff, and his men with picks, spades and barrows. George Stephenson, to his credit, was not above using Metcalf's techniques, which he did to great effect when building the Liverpool-Manchester railway over the notorious Chat Moss in Lancashire.

Most of our present main roads are ex-turnpikes, sometimes widened a little to meet the needs of modern traffic but often much the same. Surviving milestones in stone or cast-iron give the name of the old turnpike, still with the mileage to and from the starting point. In this way they differ from the pre-turnpike milestones and guide-stoops to be found at some cross roads with finger posts often marked in "customary" rather than statute miles. The present A65, which though under Ministry of Transport classification goes from Leeds to Kendal, is for the most part the old Keighley-Kendal turnpike as the milestones still indicate. Again, the lonely road that goes across the moors between Ingleton and Hawes is part of the Lancaster-Richmond turnpike.

Sometimes it is possible to trace where turnpikes have replaced older roads, and have perhaps in their turn been replaced by later turnpikes. An excellent example is at Bram-

31

hope between Bradford and Harrogate, A deep sunken land, grassy and almost hidden, is the original road—known as Staircase Lane it is now a foot and bridle path. The first turnpike, now called Old Pool Bank, climbs up from Pool very steeply to the right of the original road, and at the summit where it joins the present Leeds-Otley road—a much later highway—there is a toll-booth at Bramhope Bar. The present Bradford-Harrogate road down Pool bank is the second turnpike. Another example is the old Skipton-Addingham road, in 1780 a turnpike which must have provided coaches with a tough haul out of Skipton as it climbed steeply over Draughton Edge to the south of the existing road before descending to Addingham. It is now a straight green track and footpath, the solitude of which contrasts with the roar of traffic on the crowded road below. Only at the lane to Draughton does an old guide stoop give a clue that it was once an important road.

A few toll-booths have survived. They were often situated just outside the boundaries of a town, although sometimes in open country midway on the highway. The name "bar"

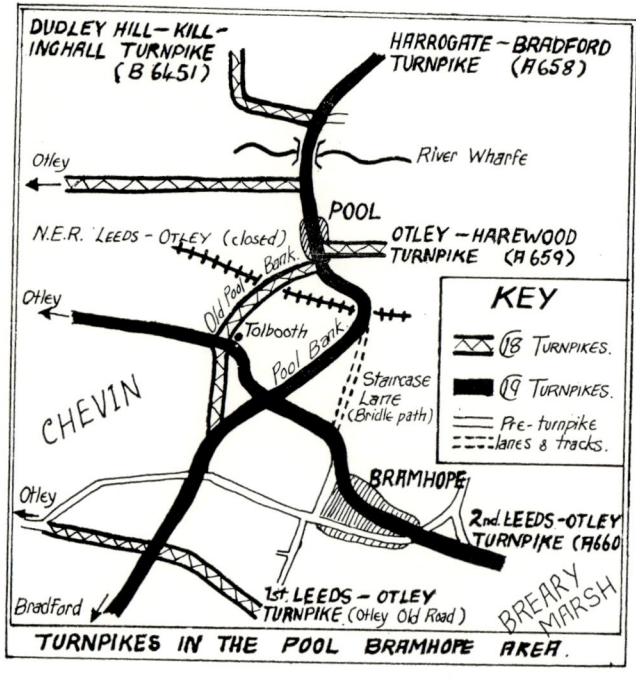

TURNPIKES IN THE POOL BRAMHOPE AREA.

Surviving toll-booth at Steanor Bottom, four miles south of Todmorden on the low-level trans-Pennine route to Rochdale. Above: general view. Right: List of tolls. (C. D. Gibbons).

often hints at their existence in a locality, and they were usually well-designed little buildings indicating the taste of the times. There is a fine square-shaped booth on the Keighley-Kendal turnpike just south of Settle, while an excellent example is now a sweet and tobacconist's shop just outside Keighley at Stocksbridge. It is in Regency style, the present shop door perhaps being the toll window, and just to the right of the shop the first milestone of the Keighley-Bradford turnpike can still be seen. Toll-booths tend to jut out slightly into the road across the pavement, and for this reason many have been demolished.

Turnpikes were not always a completely unqualified success. Some trustees were more eager to collect tolls than to pay for repairs. There was plenty of evasion of tolls, and trustees often set up gates on neighbouring roads to prevent people by-passing the toll gates. Keepers sometimes embezzled money, but by and large the general standards of roads improved quite substantially in the 18th century. In 1752 a survey of bridges which were considered repairable "at the charge of the whole West Riding" was produced, and this County Bridge Book is a fascinating record of the state of highways and bridges in the mid-18th century. By the end of the century the work of Macadam and Telford in road building and road making was greatly facilitating fast travel, and the age of coaching was dawning.

6: The Coaching Age

THE first stage coaches were operating in the London area in the 17th century and soon spread to the North. As the name implies the fare, as on a modern bus, was computed by the number of stages covered on a journey. It will be remembered how Jane Eyre, running away from Thornfield Hall, caught the stage coach at the cross-roads and travelled as far as her money would allow her. The earliest stage coaches were primitive things, hardly better than the clumsy stage wagons that lumbered between villages carrying goods, chattels and poor folk. The travelling public soon demanded better standards of comfort and improved design for the internal passengers, though it must have been pretty cold and uncomfortable for the coachmen and the outside passengers on the roof. A good example of a stage coach dating from the early 19th century is to be found at Shibden Hall, Halifax. The services soon spread throughout the country, and by the late 18th century contemporary maps showed the roads on which the coaching services were operated in the same way that a modern map might show bus routes. Operators of stage coach services and owners of inns worked extremely closely together—in fact many inn-keepers actually ran their own services.

The busiest routes were up and down the Great North Road, and to this day towns like Doncaster, Aberford, Wetherby, Boroughbridge and Catterick Bridge, spaced out at convenient intervals for coach travellers, still have their flavour of the coaching age.

New inns were specially built to accommodate the travellers, and inn-keepers did a roaring trade. A whole industry grew up around coaching; each inn required its squad of barmaids, chambermaids, cooks and waiters to attend to the travellers, while ostlers, grooms, stable-lads and smiths were there to look after the horses. Coaching inns usually had large stable yards for the coaches, and the high arched doorways—sometimes double for entrances and exits—are still to be seen all over Yorkshire, especially in the older towns. Famous old

34

inns such as the *Swan* at Aberford, the *White Horse* at Bingley (where the new extensions added to the old tavern in coaching days are evident), and the *Devonshire Arms* at Bolton Bridge on the Skipton-Harrogate turnpike, are well-known. It requires little effort to recapture the atmosphere of the old coaching days—the coachman's horn, the rattle of hooves and wheels over the cobbles, the shouts, the flurry of excitement indoors, the rush and bustle. If the old stage coaches were slow and uncomfortable by modern standards, the standard of comfort in the inns was by all accounts worse. Many 18th century writers complain about the wretched standard of country inns with landlords charging high prices for poor food and services. Fleas and bedbugs were common enough to be accepted almost without comment, and accommodation was often dirty and crowded. On the other hand many a jolly evening must have been had with a group of travellers sharing an inn for the night and swapping tales and experiences. The great 18th century novelist Henry Fielding set whole sections of his novels in coaching inns.

Travel could be perilous. Until the 19th century, roads were often grim, and it was not uncommon for coaches to overturn in the mud, to become stuck or to break an axle. An even worse hazard were highwaymen and footpads. Highwaymen often worked with inn-keepers, the landlords informing them when a likely customer was on the road, and in spite of the romantic glow which legend has given them they were quite brutal and vicious robbers. They were not just poor men, often being the dissolute sons of the aristocracy faced with drinking or gaming debts. Oxford was a notorious place for highwaymen—impoverished university students.

One of the worst places in Yorkshire for highwaymen and footpads was the Calder Valley, the narrow pass between Todmorden and Hebden Bridge surrounded by steep, dark cliffs offering plenty of shelter for robbers to descend at great speed on unlucky travellers. Robbery was so common that by the mid-18th century people were advised to tear banknotes in half when sending them through the post, dispatching each half separately to reduce the attraction to thieves. Penalties for a captured highwayman were as barbaric as suited the temper of the age; he was hanged in public and his carcase strung from a gibbet for all to see slowly rotting away. Gibbets were usually at quite prominent places and several areas have their Gibbet Hill—there is one near Knaresborough, another above Cowling and one in Halifax.

YORK Four Days Stage-Coach.

Begins on Friday the 12th. of April. 1706.

ALL that are desirous to pass from *London* to *York*, or from *York* to *London*, or any other Place on that Road; Let them Repair to the *Black Swan* in *Holbourn* in *London*, and to the *Black Swan* in *Coney street* in *York*.

At both which Places, they may be received in a Stage Coach every *Monday*, *Wednesday* and *Friday*, which performs the whole Journey in Four Days, (*if God permits.*) And sets forth at Five in the Morning.

And returns from *York* to *Stamford* in two days, and from *Stamford* by *Huntington* to *London* in two days more. And the like Stages on their return.

Allowing each Passenger 14 weight, and all above 3d. a Pound.

Performed By { Benjamin Kingman, Henry Harrison, Walter Bayne's

Also this gives Notice that Newcastle Stage Coach, sets out from York, every Monday, and Friday, and from Newcastle every Monday, and Friday.

Early coaching notice

It was to improve the speed and reliability of the mails that in the 1780s John Palmer persuaded the Walpole government to allow him to develop his mail coaches. These created new standards of postal services and passenger transport, and the phrase "post-haste" is still a tribute to Palmer's success. The mail coaches, light and tough vehicles, worked to a strict timetable, carried armed guards to deter highwaymen and took with them accurate watches which were carefully regulated with London time before departing. Until Palmer's day time was a relative affair with every small town in England having its own approximate version of Greenwich, but the new mail coaches were so reliable that villagers could usually set their clocks by the arrival of the mails. Macadam's work with road construction, using small stone chippings to create a firm surface, enabled far greater speeds to be achieved. All mails were exempt from the expense and delay of turnpike tolls, toll-keepers being fined if a mail coach was held up because of an inefficient guard. The coaches travelled day and night, only pausing briefly to change horses, and the post-horn blown by the guard indicated the passage of the mails and gave due warning to toll-keepers and stable-lads to be at the ready.

Crack services were operated along the Great North Road to Scotland, and connecting services went to and from centres en route. In 1797 the Leeds-London mail was covering the distance in 29 hours 45 minutes, and a trans-Pennine mail coach from Hull to Liverpool took 27 hours 15 minutes. The coach left Hull at 3.0 p.m. reaching York in time for an evening meal before departing to Leeds where a short halt was made. Breakfast was taken in Halifax and lunch in Manchester before reaching Liverpool at tea time. The Glasgow mails left the Great North Road at Catterick and travelled via Barnard Castle and Bowes to Appleby. There were four services a week between York and Scarborough and three between York and Whitby, both services going through Malton.

The excellence of the mail coaches caused operators of the stage services to improve their own standards. By now the turnpike network was nearing completion, and the kind of absurdity reported by Thoresby in 1714 when the Hull-York coach was only operative from May to October was disappearing. Many operators invested in what they called "flying coaches"—these were lightly built vehicles carrying less passengers and luggage and able to cover distances at greater speed. A "flying coach" of the mid-18th century covered the journey between Sheffield and London in three days with overnight

The carriage of mails by road was gradually superseded by rail in the 19th century. This Royal Mail gig operated between Arthington station and Addingham until the opening of the Ilkley-Addingham-Skipton railway in 1888. (collection of W. Overin).

stops at a fare of £1 17s, absurdly expensive by modern values. Coaches were usually recognised by their names, a practice continued in the naming of express locomotives in the railway age. The *Tally Ho* operated between Holmfirth and Huddersfield, while a busy route like Huddersfield-Leeds could boast such fine coaches as *Cornwallis, The Dart, Umpire* and *True Briton*. By 1825 the *Royal Mail* and *Royal Hope* coaches were leaving the *Packhorse Hotel*, Huddersfield, for London via Penistone. The fares were £1 11s. 6d. inside the coach and £1 1s 0d. on top, considerably in excess of equivalent first class rail fares at the present time.

The dramatic improvements which occurred in coach travel up to the dawn of the railway age can be seen by comparing times of the coaches which travelled through Yorkshire on the Great North Road between London and Edinburgh. In the 16th century coaches took between 12 and 20 days for the journey, in the 17th century 13 days, in the 18th century four days, in the early 19th century three days and two nights, and in 1833 42 hours 33 minutes. Had it not been for the development of the railways, even more spectacular improvements in these times would have been possible. Urged by the growth of road transport, Thomas Telford surveyed a new highway between London and Northumberland to replace the Great North Road. He spent nearly five years on the survey between 1824 and 1829, and the work was almost complete when news arrived of a semi-literate Northumberland mining engineer's brilliant feats with machines known as steam locomotives. It was almost another 150 years before Telford's vision of a fine new highway to the north, albeit only as far as Leeds, came into being. We call it the M.1.

ROSE & CROWN INN, and GENERAL COACH OFFICE, Top of BRIGGATE, LEEDS.
Very REDUCED FARES from LEEDS to HULL, by Way of KNOTTINGLEY and GOOLE, also from WAKEFIELD to HULL by the same Route.

The Inhabitants of Leeds, Hull, Wakefield, and the Public are most respectfully informed that WILLIAM THE FOURTH COACH, leaves the above Inn every Morning at Five o'Clock, (Sundays excepted,) by Way of Castleford and Pontefract; the QUEEN ADELAIDE COACH leaves the Strafford Arms Inn, Wakefield, at a Quarter-past Five; and both reach Knottingley at Seven o'Clock, whence the Passengers are immediately forwarded by the TWIN PACKET to Goole, Drawn by Four Horses, where they arrive by Ten o'Clock, in Time to join the STEAM PACKET for Hull.

Passengers by this Line of Packets possess therefore a great Advantage, by avoiding the Delay so frequent by grounding between Selby and Goole.

FARES

	s.	d.
From Leeds to Hull Inside Coach, and Best Cabin	6	0
Ditto to Goole, ditto	4	0
Ditto to Knottingley, Inside	3	6
Ditto to Hull, Outside Coach and Best Cabin	5	0
Ditto to Goole ditto	3	6
Ditto to Hull Outside, and Fore Cabin	4	0
Ditto to Goole ditto	3	0
Ditto to Knottingley, Outside	2	6
Ditto to Castleford, Inside	3	0
Ditto to Castleford, Outside	2	0

Fares from Wakefield in Proportion.

To those who have tried this Mode of Conveyance, it will be unnecessary to point out its superior Advantages; to Others it may be needful to state, that the TWIN PACKETS are neatly fitted up, with every Requisite for the Accommodation and Comfort of Passengers; Refreshments, &c. are provided in a superior Style; and no Care or Expense is or will be spared to render this Line of Conveyance worthy of that extensive Support which the Proprietors have already received, and for which they beg to tender their most grateful Thanks.

The coaches are driven by careful, experienced, and attentive Drivers. The TWIN PACKET travels Seven Miles an Hour, and the mode of Conveyance ensures the greatest regularity.

Passengers to Askern Spa, are accommodated with a CAR direct from Heck Bridge to that celebrated Watering Place.—Also, a CAR from KNOTTINGLEY to any of the Neighbouring Villages.

Performed by the Public's most obedient Servants,
FRANCIS & COATES,
ROBERT EARNSHAW,
THOMAS DUNNILL & CO.

Leeds, August 17th, 1832.

Travel advertisement of 1832, when the journey from Leeds to Hull involved a combination of stage-coach and steam packet.

7: The Canal Era

WATER transport has always been extremely important in Yorkshire with its long coastline and major rivers, notably the Ouse and Humber, which from ancient times allowed trade to be developed. In days when land transport by pack-horse or crude wagon was slow, unreliable and expensive, the sooner the goods could be water-borne the better. There are good scientific reasons for this as the amount of energy required, be it paddle, sail or horse, to haul a load on water is a fraction of that required to haul the same on land. A horse that can pull one ton weight in a road cart can pull three tons in a railway wagon, but if the load is in a boat and there is no contrary current the same beast can haul a fantastic 27 tons.

It is not surprising that a large number of our major cities have grown up on navigable waterways, and many of them are in fact inland ports. Leeds was almost the highest point to which the Aire was navigable, Sheffield the Don, and York the Ouse, while Hull owes its prominence to the Humber. From medieval times the value of the waterways was realised as trade expanded. In 1462 Edward IV appointed the mayor and aldermen of York conservators of the rivers Aire, Derwent, Wharfe, Don, Humber and Ouse, and Acts passed by Cromwell and William III gave further powers for improving navigation.

There was always a conflict between people who travelled up and down rivers—from earliest times rights of way—and people who lived on them, in particular those who built dams and weirs to hold back previously shallow waters in order to drive a waterwheel. The history of rivers is full of bitter quarrels between mill-owners and river authorities over the construction of weirs. Acts were passed in 1697 and 1700 to keep the Aire and Calder navigable, the government as usual supporting the merchant interests, and from then Leeds began to grow into a commercial centre. Coastal shipping was always an important means of transportation in Britain, particularly when roads were so bad, and it was clearly much easier to unload a vessel at Hull or York into smaller barges than transport large loads to inland centres. It was soon clear that rivers in

Yorkshire could only be kept navigable by careful management, by dredging, by repairing and supporting banks. With skilled management it is surprising how far inland commercial boats could reach—Yarm, Boroughbridge and Beverley were all important inland ports in Tudor times, while York owed its ever greater dominance in the later Middle Ages to the Ouse.

As manufacturing industries began to develop in South and West Yorkshire, and larger and larger quantities of material needed to be transported—particularly for the growing iron industries—existing rivers began to prove inadequate. The Calder was improved as far as Wakefield by the late 17th century, while the company of cutlers in Sheffield improved the Don to allow barges to reach Doncaster carrying 30 tons and Sheffield carrying 20 tons. A company known as "The Proprietors of the Navigation of the river Dun" ("Dun" is an alternative and other form of "Don") was formed to finance cuts to avoid difficult parts of the river and enable even larger barges to serve the upper reaches. During the 18th century the waterway was increasingly developed, giving the iron-masters of Sheffield direct access by boat to Hull and London, and also allowing cheap coal to be brought in great quantities from the Yorkshire coalfield. Further west the mill-owners of the West Riding, realising the importance of cheap bulk transport to enable their industries to expand, developed the rivers Aire, Calder and Hebble, and formed the Aire and Calder and Calder and Hebble Navigation companies to enable the necessary improvements to take place.

Gradually the idea crystallised of building entirely new stretches of waterway to allow vessels to pass without encountering difficult hazards or strong currents. As always the Romans had been first with their Foss Dyke in Lincolnshire while locks on short cuts were well known—the earliest example was built in the 16th century near Exeter. These early locks were what is known as flash locks; simply weirs with removable tops. The boat would float over the weir in the rush of water when the top was removed, but it was evidently a hazardous business.

One strong stimulus to the building of canals was the cost of coal. The steam engine, which was being developed to drive the mills of the West Riding, needed enormous quantities of cheap coal. It was the genius of one man which largely brought the canal age into being. James Brindley, engineer to the Duke of Bridgewater, built his celebrated canal on the Duke's

41

Atmosphere of the canal age.   A steam barge on the Springs Branch of the Leeds and Liverpool canal at Skipton (Alexander Keighley).

estate between Worsley and Manchester. It was done with amazing speed, the Act being passed in 1759 and the canal opened in 1761 . In building the Bridgewater Canal, Brindley constructed one of the wonders of the age in the amazing Barton aqueduct over the Mersey, but his achievement was impressive in another way for it halved the price of the Duke's coal and brought great wealth to the Duke himself. The news soon echoed round England, and the resultant excitement and release of energy is now seen as the start of the industrial revolution.

It is absurd to regard the enormous complex of social and technological changes which were occurring at the end of the 18th century as the result of a single happening, for the industrial revolution was taking place from the late Middle Ages onwards and, in a very real sense, is still continuing.

But it is possible to see one event as igniting the touch paper and triggering off enormous forces that had been slowly building up. Brindley and his friends did more than anyone else to change the face of England and to allow the growing technological sophistication of the age to be harnessed. The enormous upsurge of activity that produced the wealth and power of Victorian England, which spread throughout Western Europe and the World, came about with the creation of the canals. It is odd that these dull, drab, forgotten strips of water, the gloomy mould-green wharves and towpaths usually in the most squalid parts of towns and cities, were the beginnings of all our power and affluence. They have made modern Yorkshire possible.

Brindley's triumphs in south Lancashire soon awakened hopes and ambitions across the Pennines. The first effort was to extend the Ure to Ripon by means of some short sections of canal and improvements to the navigation from Borough-bridge, but a much more extensive scheme was soon proposed to connect Leeds with the port of Liverpool by a canal across England. Mr. John Longbotham of Halifax had already surveyed a possible route when the great James Brindley was called in to give his view. He confirmed Longbotham's route, and as by this time he had several other commitments Long-botham was placed in charge of the project. In 1766 a meeting was called in Bradford and the project launched. The new company soon had the sanction of Parliament to build the canal and by 1773 the Bingley-Skipton section was opened. The canal was in use from Leeds to Holmbridge, near Gargrave, in 1777. Longbotham shared Brindley's aversion to natural obstacles, and chose the longer route round the Aire Gap rather than face expensive locking and tunnelling problems. Nevertheless there were many difficulties.

There were quite a lot of bridges and embankments to be built, and some fairly steep gradients. Longbotham used the "staircase" method of locking, several locks being built together in a single unit in order to save costs. The most famous example is the celebrated Bingley "Five Rise" locks, still a wonderful piece of canal engineering, where Longbotham made use of a convenient Pennine stream to save water and a complex system of sluices to obviate the need for a separate feed reservoir. The only disadvantage of "staircase" operation is that at busy times it can create rather a bottleneck. There was a long delay before work was started on the central section of the canal. Robert Whitworth, who took over from Longbotham, preferred the more direct methods which were then fashionable and drove a tunnel through Foulridge near Colne. It was a tunnel well-named when barges were operated by steam power. Expense delayed the completion of the canal for several more years and it was left to a third engineer, Fletcher, to finish building the 127-miles long waterway in 1816, 46 years after the original Act of Parliament.

Today it is the only surviving trans-Pennine canal in navigable condition, but although it is officially classed as "open" by British Waterways, commercial traffic is just about non-existent on the Yorkshire section. In recent years the use by pleasure craft has however grown considerably. It is a broad canal, that is 14 feet wide as opposed to a narrow canal of 7-feet width, and its locks are capable of taking boats up to 60-feet long carrying loads of up to 50 tons. Narrow canals, although accommodating longer boats, carried much less, their main advantages being cheapness of construction and economy in water which was important when canals ran through hilly areas. It is not without significance that narrow canals have fared less well in recent times, and most in Yorkshire are closed.

What was the effect of the Leeds-Liverpool canal on the communities along it? It was a great feat of engineering, and

Mills hugged the banks of canals as shown by this aerial view of Titus Salt's mill at Saltaire. The river Aire is in the left foreground, the Leeds and Liverpool canal runs from the top left to the bottom right corner, and the railway is immediately behind the large chimney (Aero Pictorial Ltd.).

The tiny Marsden entrance to Standedge canal tunnel—longest and highest in Britain. Behind it are the railway tunnels (Colin Speakman).

is a moving tribute to the thousands of anonymous navvies who built it with shovel and pick-axe. They were men from the remote Dales villages, from Scotland, Devon and Ireland, living in rough settlements and shanty towns while they drove the cut through the clays and millstone grit of the Pennines. There was a fair amount of hostility at times from landowners, but the commercial benefits of the canal were too attractive for this to be sustained. In the early days it seemed the waterway might well be a passenger carrier in addition to conveying quantities of cheap coal. It cost 3s. 6d. to travel by barge between Leeds and Skipton, but the journey must have taken all day for horse-drawn barges averaged only about four miles an hour. The real impact of the canal was the impetus given to the manufacturing towns along the Aire valley. Bradford soon had its arm of the canal, and towns such as Shipley, Bingley, Keighley and Skipton grew and prospered. The mills hugged the bank like beads on a string; an example is Titus Salt's mill at Saltaire with wharves which must have once been alive with activity. Raw materials from Liverpool and coal and iron from south Yorkshire arrived by the bargeload, and the barges went away with fine woollens destined for Liverpool, Hull, Europe, the United States and the Colonies. The wealth of Yorkshire travelled by barge.

By 1784 Huddersfield was connected with the Calder by Sir John Ramsden's $3\frac{1}{2}$-mile Huddersfield broad canal—the initial cost was £11,794 and this was recouped by a toll of 1s. 6d. per ton load. Two of the most daring ventures through the Pennines were both financial failures. The first of these was the Huddersfield narrow canal, extending for 20 miles from Huddersfield to the Ashton Canal with which it con-

YORKSHIRE'S NAVIGABLE RIVERS

nected near Manchester. It was the highest summit (644-feet) and the longest tunnel (Standedge, 5,416-feet) of any canal in Great Britain. That tunnel—running from Marsden to Diggle —was an incredible feat, being constructed by pick and dynamite over a period of thirteen years between 1798 and 1811. The canal cost £300,000 and never really justified its expense. It was opened with much pomp and ceremony, but the tunnel was always a difficulty. Barges were "legged" through as there was no tow-path; men had to lie on their backs and propel the barge by digging their feet into the low roof and pushing. It must have been an agonising task. There were professional "leggers" to help tired bargemen, and occasionally vagrants would work their passage on a barge

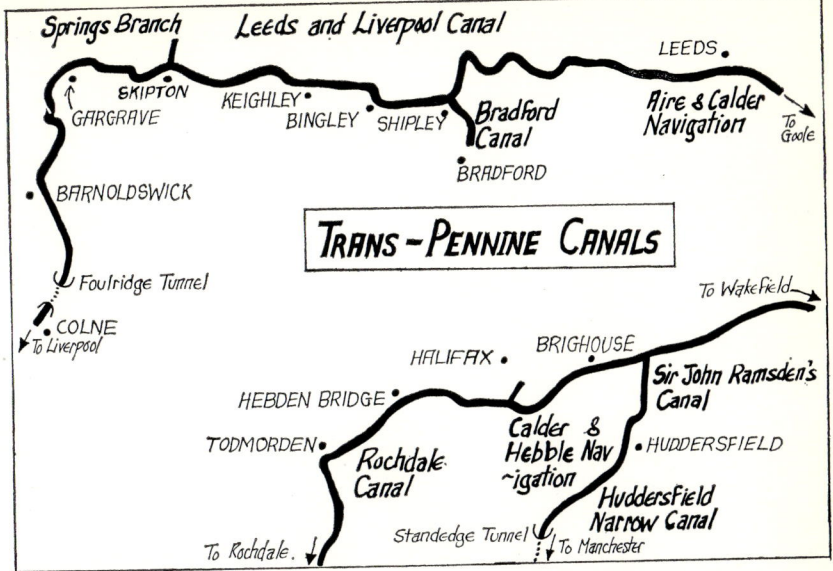

The canal network of Yorkshire. Opposite page: The extensive system of navigable rivers and canals connecting with the Humber estuary. Above: Trans-Pennine canals.

by helping to "leg" through the tunnel. The canal was closed in 1944, the locks "weired" and the tunnel mouth gated. People do sometimes get permission to make the nightmarish journey through but it must be like a trip down Hades. The tunnel entrances at Diggle and at Marsden are still worth a visit; the tunnel is appallingly narrow, a small and dark hole through the sheer rock face with the two railway tunnels running parallel to it. When these were built—the first of them by the Huddersfield and Manchester Railway and Canal Company in the 1840s—their construction was a relatively simple affair for, thanks to the canal tunnel, material was simply loaded on to waiting barges. Access holes still exist between the railway and the canal tunnel, which must have been suffocating when a steam engine went through.

A magnificent failure of the canal age was John Rennie's Rochdale Canal, first promoted in 1794 and going through the Todmorden gap into Calderdale to meet the Calder and Hebble Navigation and provide a much more direct trans-Pennine link than the Leeds and Liverpool Canal. The route called for all Rennie's considerable skill; it had to be blasted through hard millstone grit along the narrow valley, over 90

Locks on the Leeds and Liverpool canal. The three left-hand views are at Barrowford on the west side of Foulridge tunnel; the right-hand photographs depict Barnoldswick locks (David Joy).

locks were required and a complex system of reservoirs and pumps had to be built to counterbalance the inevitable shortage of water when several barges passed through. In spite of Rennie's genius the canal always suffered from this chronic water shortage, but it deserves a better fate than its present scandalous neglect. It was abandoned some years ago and is now a pathetic rotting drain, a muddy little sump for bicycle wheels and old washing-up-liquid bottles. Rennie's canal could still be a beautiful and useful amenity to the people of the upper Calder valley.

The boatmen of Yorkshire's canals have all but vanished. Originally day-boats were often the means of working shifts using barges, men and horses in relays. As railway competition grew the houseboat system was generally adopted; a boatman and his wife would tend a couple of boats, the second or trailer boat being the houseboat. It was an interesting if tough way of life, with a whole family living in the tiny space of a barge. There was a touch of the Romany about them, boats being decorated in highly individualistic ways to form a folk art of the canals. Railway and later road competition has driven the boatmen away, while such problems as the schooling of children made life difficult and inconvenient. A few rotting barges can be found here and there, some converted to house-boats, and there are still fine old lock-keepers' cottages long since deserted and canal inns such as the famous *Rodley Barge* at Rodley or the *Anglers' Arms* at Bingley. One or two canal men can be found. I have an old friend who has worked all his life on the Leeds and Liverpool Canal, and is one of the handful of men employed to maintain the lock gates and do minor repairs. He still contends that the lack of commercial craft on the canal is "all a railway plot." I think he takes a certain pleasure in noting the steady increase of week-end trippers on the canal while the nearby once powerful railway declines.

He has a point. The railways, once they were built, not only exploited their huge natural advantages over the canal companies but seemed brutally determined to eradicate even the feeblest competition. The Lancashire & Yorkshire and the London & North-Western railways acquired a 25-year lease of the tolls of the Leeds and Liverpool Canal, and immediately raised them to prohibitive levels. A similar fate befell the Rochdale Canal. The railways eventually relented but too late. Perhaps a more fundamental failure was the inability of the canal companies to adapt to the new age. The mixture of broad and narrow canals was often an inconvenient expense, while in the Pennines water tended to be short in dry seasons. There was no money for investment, and although steam and petrol engines ultimately superseded horses the waterways simply failed to hold their own.

The Inland Waterways Association, who have rightly advocated the retention of our canal system, have in the past often suggested that it could still be made commercially viable as are the Continental waterways. This may be so, but I doubt if our Pennine canals could ever be really profitable. Would it then be better to fill them in as some people, looking at the dereliction that has overcome many of them, have suggested? The answer is definitely not. First of all it would cost an enor-mous amount of money, while risks to children have been exaggerated. Secondly they provide a lot of water for various industrial concerns; a quite large revenue comes to the Water-ways Board from this source. Most important of all, though, is their value for leisure.

In the last quarter of the 20th century leisure is likely to be an increasingly important consideration. More people will have more free time, and the waterways of Yorkshire are already a priceless asset. Hundreds of people make their way to the canals at week-ends to fish the shallow waters. One cannot however easily cost their value for this alone and increasingly people are taking up leisure cruising. In towns like Leeds, Bradford and Halifax which are a long way inland, the easiest way to take a pleasant cruise is to hire or buy a boat on the local canal, and in this way their use is growing. The quietness, peace and beauty of the old canals has come as a revelation to many people, while the towpaths are also a valuable asset. Pleasant walks exist alongside the Leeds & Liverpool Canal, for instance, around Gargrave and East Marton where the Gisburn road crosses over that strange double-arch bridge. Other possibilities exist along the high level section above Silsden; around Saltaire and Bingley where the river and canal at one point run parallel through a lovely wooded valley; along the thickly-wooded section around Esholt, Apperley and Calverley; or even around Armley and Kirkstall close to the centre of Leeds. With a little skilful planning, a piazza or two, some paint, the clearing of rubbish, a few benches and some trees, Leeds or the "backs" of Shipley could possess their own little Venices.

The Transport Act of 1968 demonstrated the Government's intention to develop many canals as Cruiseways—waterways open for leisure purposes, boating, walking and fishing—and recent plans announced that money was to be spent on improving certain waterways, including the Leeds and Liverpool Canal, for this purpose. There is talk of creating linear parks along the canal and riversides in Leeds, and with skill and care and perhaps some voluntary labour they could be made into places of beauty. There is another important point. Our canals are rich in history, and we ought to be proud of the fact that in the West Riding the industrial revolution which changed the world first came into being. The lock gates and machinery are fascinating relics of early industrial technology, and lock-keepers' cottages, warehouses and bridges are often fine examples of architecture in their own right.

8: The Railway Age

THE earliest railways were very primitive affairs. Wagon-ways were probably well-known in Roman and certainly in monastic times, the earliest simply being lengths of rough timber laid down near the entrance of a mine to stop the wheels of the little pit wagons sinking into the mud. Gradually the idea of flanged wheels running on wooden rails developed, a couple of horses hauling the long "train" to a point where the ore or coal could be loaded onto a barge or ship. The next stage, where usage was heavy, was to bolt strips of iron to the wood, as on a clog, to prevent the surface from being worn away. In 1776 John Curr, a Sheffield ironmaster, laid down flanged rails on which wagons with flangeless wheels operated, but this development was in the wrong direction and went out of general favour after little more than 25 years.

Yorkshire has particular claim to be one of the pioneer counties in the development of railways. In 1758 Charles Brandling obtained the first railway Act of Parliament to construct a wooden wagonway, running from his colliery at Middleton and across Hunslet Moor to the city of Leeds. This historic line, the Middleton Railway, is now preserved and operated by the Middleton Railway Trust and still carries commercial traffic. Although the first public line authorised by Parliament was possibly the Surrey Iron Railway in 1804, the Middleton Railway was the scene of important developments in the work of its two great engineers, John Blenkinsop and Matthew Murray. Blenkinsop, clearly highly impressed with Trevithick's experimental steam locomotive, developed his own successful designs. Two of the most notable were *Salamanca* and *Prince Regent*, engines working on the rack and pinion principle, which astonished onlookers in 1812 hauling a train of 38 wagons at 3 m.p.h. across Hunslet Moor. This line, the first successful steam-operated railway in the world, quickly became famous and pit managers and their engineers came from far and wide to see Blenkinsop's engines. George Stephenson, then an unknown young engine-wright from Killingworth High Pit in Northumberland was one of them. Always a brilliant borrower of others' ideas, as well as having a profoundly original engineering mind himself, he

The Middleton Railway at Leeds was the first to be built by Act of Parliament and later became the first rack railway in the world employing the first locomotives to be used commercially on a flanged rail. This view was engraved by N. Whittock.

realised that a few simple modifications could improve the performances of the machines. He went home to experiment; the steam age was born.

Though the Stockton & Darlington Railway is just over the county boundary, its history is relevant to the development of Yorkshire railways. At that time there was a great public debate on methods of improving communications between the Durham mining areas, and in particular the town of Darlington and the Tees port of Stockton. The great canal engineer, Rennie, had already surveyed a canal but the cost was prohibitive. There was support in the town for the idea of building a railway between the two centres and Stephenson, whose reputation was already growing, was called in. After a protracted public debate the rail lobby was victorious and the "father of railways" set to work. Stephenson's solving of the many complex engineering problems has become legendary. As a pioneer facing many unknowns his work was hazardous and difficult, but the line was opened for passengers in 1825.

It is important to remember that the Stockton & Darlington company in its initial stages operated like a canal company or a turnpike trust, intending to make money out of tools. As a result a great variety of traffic was operated in the early years. Steam locomotives hauled trains of carriages which were largely open wagons or coaches roughly adapted to fit on flat wagons, but many operators still used horses and a sort of stage coach or horse tram trundling along the lines. As the line was single track for most of the way and had few passing places, the results were often chaotic with frequent obstructions. Steam usually had preference, and on at least one occasion when locomotive and horse-coach met on the line face to face the unfortunate passengers had to descend from their coach and lift it bodily from the line. Eventually the company decided to close the line to all but their own traffic in order to organise a more rational state of affairs, and finally all trains became steam hauled.

There was initially a fair amount of opposition. Landowners resisted the railway, especially when they experienced the din and "sulphurous fumes" of the engines, but its commercial success was so fantastic that it soon drew the claws of any opposition. New prosperity came to both towns which, in spite of Stockton's fears, did not diminish when the line was extended to Middlesbrough in 1830. The idea was to have a much larger port further down the Tees. Middlesbrough before that time was just a minute village, but almost overnight it became a boom town. Yorkshire had the first town in England whose creation and development was the direct result of the new railway age, and the development was given fresh impetus a few years later when rich deposits of iron ore were found in the nearby Cleveland hills.

Yorkshire merchants were not slow to realise the enormous advantages which a railway could bestow on their own trade. The port of Hull was watching with some apprehension the success of its rival Goole, and feared loss of trade unless communications between the West Riding and itself were improved. It was decided to build a railway over the most difficult stretch as far as Selby to connect with the Hull boats. In 1830 the Leeds & Selby Railway was formed, the engineer in charge being James Walker. In spite of difficulties, including a 200-yard tunnel through Richmond Hill just outside Leeds and a bridge which caused some problems near Garforth, the line was opened in 1834. Double track all the way, it commenced at the first Leeds station in Marsh Lane. The opening train was packed with local dignitaries, and over 20,000 people turned up to watch the great event. The little engine, the *Nelson*, struggled under the load up the steep incline out of Leeds, barely reaching walking pace. It took 1 hour 10 minutes to cover the first $4\frac{1}{2}$ miles. This was hardly a promising beginning, but once on the level it shot away at a sensational 20 m.p.h.

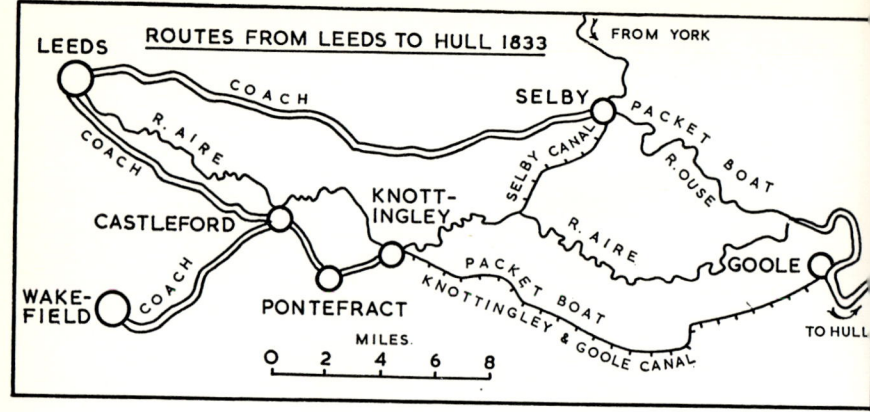

ROUTES FROM LEEDS TO HULL 1833

Morning and afternoon trains were operated, special omnibuses carrying passengers from Kirkgate to Marsh Lane for fourpence. The fare from Leeds to Selby was 3s. first class and 2s second class. At Selby passengers continued their journey by the Selby Packet Company's vessels to Hull, although the voyage was not always uneventful. Departures were dependent on the state of the Humber tides, and it is recorded that there were delays, with passengers even being forced to help to rock the boat off shallows when the captain had underestimated the depth of the river. In the first four days 779 passengers travelled by the railway, and this was no mere rush of novelty interest. By 1835 some 3,500 passengers a week were being carried as opposed to about a previous 400 a week by coach. This was indeed a transport revolution. It was soon realised that the break of journey was far from ideal. In 1834 a separate company, the Hull & Selby, was formed and the through line between Leeds and Hull was opened in 1840.

By now there was frenzied activity all over the country. Two important lines had been initiated—the Great North of England to build a line from York to Darlington and the powerful York & North Midland to form a link with other lines in the Midlands with a view to eventually reaching London. By 1839 the York & North Midland had made a connection with the Leeds & Selby allowing journeys to be made between Leeds, Hull and York. The old station at York was constructed in 1841.

A particularly interesting old line was the Whitby & Pickering. The old port of Whitby, concerned at keeping its prosperity in an age of new rivals, realised its communications with the hinterland needed to be improved. A canal was initially

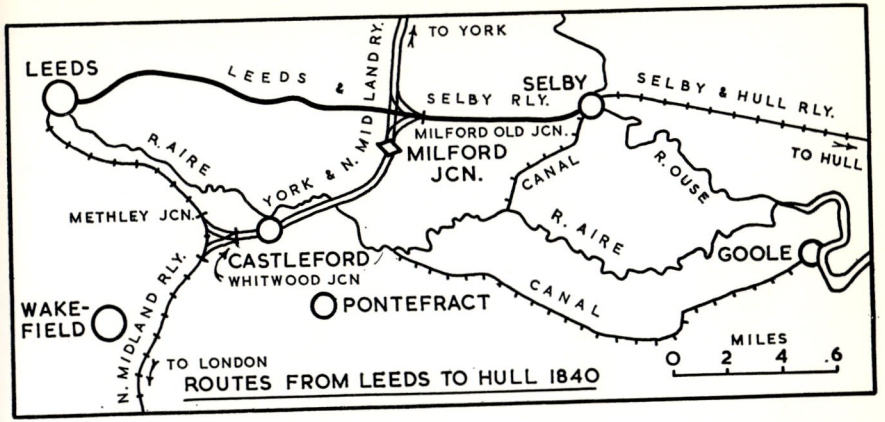

ROUTES FROM LEEDS TO HULL 1840

considered and then a railway. A route was surveyed via Kildale and Stokesley, but the cost was enormous and the advice of George Stephenson was sought. Stephenson immediately saw the valley of Newtondale as the perfect natural solution, and recommended a railway to Pickering. The route, 24 miles long, was opened in 1836. It was originally entirely horse-drawn, traffic at first not seeming to justify the expense of steam engines. The greatest difficulty in the line's construction was at the Whitby end of the narrow Esk valley where several bridges were required, while at Beckhole near Grosmont a cruel 1 in 15 incline confronted Stephenson. The cheapest and simplest way of overcoming this was a haulage system of ropes and water-balances. Passengers were hauled up one coach at a time, taking refreshment while they waited for the train to be re-assembled before departing down Newtondale to Pickering. One amusing feature of early operation on the line was the dandy-carts in which the horses rested when the trains were descending. Steam locomotives were introduced in 1847, specially powerful engines being designed for the steep and winding line which was acquired by the York & North Midland Railway. Following a nasty accident a new and less steep route was constructed between Grosmont and Goathland.

The line, an early and much regretted victim of the Beeching Axe, is in the process of being acquired by the North Yorkshire Moors Railway Preservation Society, and it is hoped that it will soon become a living museum of steam locomotives and old rolling stock with regular services again being operated. It is still possible to visit the old Beckhole incline which is a fascinating place. From Grosmont station the footpath running parallel to the Pickering line is Stephenson's route of 1836; the abutments of the old bridge remain and the narrow tunnel is the original bore. At Beckhole it is easy to pick up the railway again through the village. The building at the bottom of the incline is still called Incline Cottage and in the garden is a short piece of original iron rail on its stone-block sleepers. The incline provides a pleasant stroll, the cottages at the top being old station buildings.

It is difficult now to understand the incredible and naive excitements that early railways created. Suddenly whole new vistas of travel and experience were opened up; for 19th century man it was the most spectacular technological breakthrough possible. Fast and cheap communications, with railway fares soon being a fraction of coach fares, unified the nation in a way that was never before thought likely. Ideas, information and materials, exchanged with railway speed, altered the whole way of life of the British people—including Yorkshire people. For the first time large numbers of folk discovered the country-side for pleasure, while rural dwellers were able to see the towns. The face of Yorkshire was changing more dramatically and swiftly than ever before. The process had begun with the canals, for without them the railways could never have developed at the speed they did. Railways prospered because the great coal and iron industries were there to supply the initial materials, and it was the canals that had allowed these industries to develop. The process of industrialisation is a continuum, but its pace had accelerated to a remarkable degree. No one, not even in the remotest corner of the Dales or the Wolds, could be unaware of the fact that a new age had dawned.

The railway revolution brought its hazards. Frenzied and idiotic speculation broke out, there being a naive belief that a railway was the cure for all economic ills. Many hare-brained schemes were doomed before they began, and there were disastrous failures. Who better epitomises the spirit of the age than that splendid blend of genius, visionary and fraud, George Hudson? Chairman of the York & North Midland, and several other companies, "King" Hudson was the wonder of the age. With incredible energy and daring he launched one brilliant scheme after another—schemes which laid the foundations of Yorkshire's rail network for the next hundred years. For a time his word was law. His Great North of England Railway had by this time extended to Newcastle, and had plans to continue to the Scottish Border and Edin-

TO HULL AND BACK THE SAME DAY.
GOOD FRIDAY,
BY RAILWAY AND STEAM PACKET.

THE PUBLIC are informed that Arrangements have been made for carrying Passengers to HULL and BACK, *on Friday, the Thirteenth Instant,* also to Booth Ferry, Howden Dike, or any other intermediate Places. The Train will leave the Depot, Marsh Lane, at SEVEN in the MORNING, and Parties will arrive in Hull by Packet about One o'Clock. The Packet will leave Hull again about Five and arrive in Leeds by Railway at Ten. Fares to Hull and back,—

First Class and Best Cabin .... 9s.
Second Ditto and Common Ditto .... 6s.

WILLIAM SIMPSON, Superintendent.

Railway Office, April 6th, 1838.

Advertisement for a day-trip from Leeds to Hull on Good Friday, 1838—one of the first railway excursions on record.

burgh. The York & North Midland had acquired the Leeds & Selby and was constructing a line to Harrogate via Church Fenton with the intention of joining the Great North of England line coming southwards from Pilmoor to Boroughbridge.

The Hudson empire extended northwards from York to Scarborough, putting the famous Yorkshire resort in close contact with huge numbers of potential visitors and establishing its importance. It was typical of Hudson that on the first day of operation on the line he should offer free rides for all to bring the crowds in. A connection was built to the Whitby & Pickering Railway from Malton, and he also developed the lines from Hull to Beverley and Bridlington and from York and Selby to Market Weighton. Hudson's methods—to put it mildly—were just a little unscrupulous even by the very generous standards of the 19th century. He frequently juggled with capital, using one company's money to pay another company's debts and selling property from one company to another at a handsome profit to himself. When the railway boom proved not quite as splendid as Hudson had hoped, many of these dealings came to light and Hudson resigned amid a scandal that shocked the nation. Prices of shares fell to rock bottom, fortunes were lost, and gloom and misery settled over the land. Recovery soon followed but Hudson was a ruined man. In spite of his ruthless self-interest he had sufficient vision to see that the future of Britain's railways lay not in little local routes but in a national network, and he forged the way to creating the huge and powerful companies which made this possible.

In 1854 a group of companies in the North amalgamated in this manner. They included Hudson's own York & North Midland, the York, Newcastle & Berwick (formed by a union of the Great North of England and the Newcastle & Berwick), and the Leeds Northern formerly known as the Leeds & Thirsk. This last was formed in 1845 by the citizens of Leeds, who feared that Hudson was establishing York as a railway centre to the detriment of their own town which was being denied a direct route to the North. The line, opened in 1849, was expensive to build requiring huge viaducts over the Aire and Wharfe, and embankments and cuttings at the approaches to Bramhope tunnel. This tunnel, still the eighth longest in Britain, was an immense undertaking. Twenty-three men died in its construction, and a model of the tunnel as a memorial to them stands in Otley churchyard. It is said that opposition from Alwoodley landowners, who feared for their fox-hunting, caused the tracks to be built in this direction instead of by the less steep route to the east. The line is the present Leeds-Harrogate railway, the northern section being closed.

The companies which amalgamated in 1854 formed themselves into the North Eastern Railway, a monopoly that dominated Yorkshire's transport for 70 years and was one of the richest and best managed lines in the kingdom. Further routes were opened to serve most of the North and East Ridings, and powerful new locomotives built by men like the Worsdells and Raven set high standards. Close co-operation with the Great Northern and North British railways soon led to the London-Edinburgh "East Coast" route being developed in close rivalry with the West Coast and the Midland routes to the North and Scotland.

Travel in the early years, the 1830s and 1840s, must have been grim. First class passengers enjoyed stage-coach type carriages, but second and third class had to contend with open trucks. Engines were noisy, dirty and hopelessly unreliable in

The splendour of the steam age captures two young admirers. An express thunders over the 21-arch viaduct spanning the river Wharfe at Arthington (S. E. Ross).

spite of occasional bursts of impressive speed. Explosions were not infrequent, and when in 1837 the Royal Mail was transferred from coaches to the railways postal services lost much in reliability for a year or two. With experience standards improved. An Act of 1844 set up certain minimum standards for all trains, establishing a uniform 4ft 8½ins gauge, a guaranteed service from every station at the rate of a penny per mile (the Victorian "Parliamentary" train), and basic standards of convenience and comfort—although basic was the word. Corridor trains and accessible toilets were still a long way off, so minimum stops were compulsory for such purposes. I remember when steam engines still operated the old Carlisle "slow," crawling down to Hellifield and resting their limbs for a full 15 minutes. I believe that was still a "Parliamentary" stop, and this was in the early 1960s!

Even as late as 1860 passengers were advised to carry their own lamps on rail journeys. It was the Midland Railway that really brought tolerable standards of comfort to passengers.

59

The Midland was the product of an amalgamation of a group of competing companies in the densely populated Nottingham-Derby-Sheffield area, rich in coal mining and industry. The line reached Leeds via Normanton, and the acquisition of the Leeds & Bradford Railway provided a much-needed link towards the North. The Leeds & Bradford, one of Hudson's old companies, was opened in the 1840s to serve the Aire Valley and by 1847 had thrown out an arm from Shipley to Skipton. It was used by Elizabeth Gaskell and Anne and Charlotte Brontë soon after its opening, on the occasion of Anne's last desperate bid to cure her consumption at Scarborough. From Skipton the Midland used and later purchased the "little" North-Western Railway to Ingleton where, after an awkward change of trains, passengers could continue to Scotland. The Midland was the first railway to abolish second class accommodation and create new standards of comfort for all passengers, both third and first. The best first class coaches on the Midland were by any standards superb; a sumptuous dining car survives in the Transport Museum at Clapham, London. Pullman cars were also first introduced on the Midland.

With the acquisition of its own route into London culminating with the opening in 1868 of the massive Gothic Revival palace known as St. Pancras station, the Midland was desperate for its own route to Scotland. It was tired of having to rely on using the inconvenient connections provided by its rival, the London & North-Western. This aim was finally achieved by driving a railway through the wildest and loneliest section of the Pennines. The Settle-Carlisle line was a heroic piece of engineering. The natural obstacles were formidable, the climate wild and wet for most of the year, but the Midland was determined to build the line almost regardless of expense. An army of navvies living in shanty towns constructed what was to be the most difficult and expensive railway in Britain, and one of the last made entirely by manual labour. The line is on a gigantic scale with huge viaducts, cuttings, tunnels, sturdily constructed bridges, earthworks and stations. It is not only the highest main line in England; it is surely the most beautiful, climbing up North Ribblesdale under the shoulder of Whernside, along the head of Dentdale and Garsdale and over Ais Gill to the glorious Eden Valley. It is a magnificent, surviving tribute to Victorian engineering at its most expansive; it has a grandeur in its construction that matches the landscape.

The expansion of the Midland increased the importance of

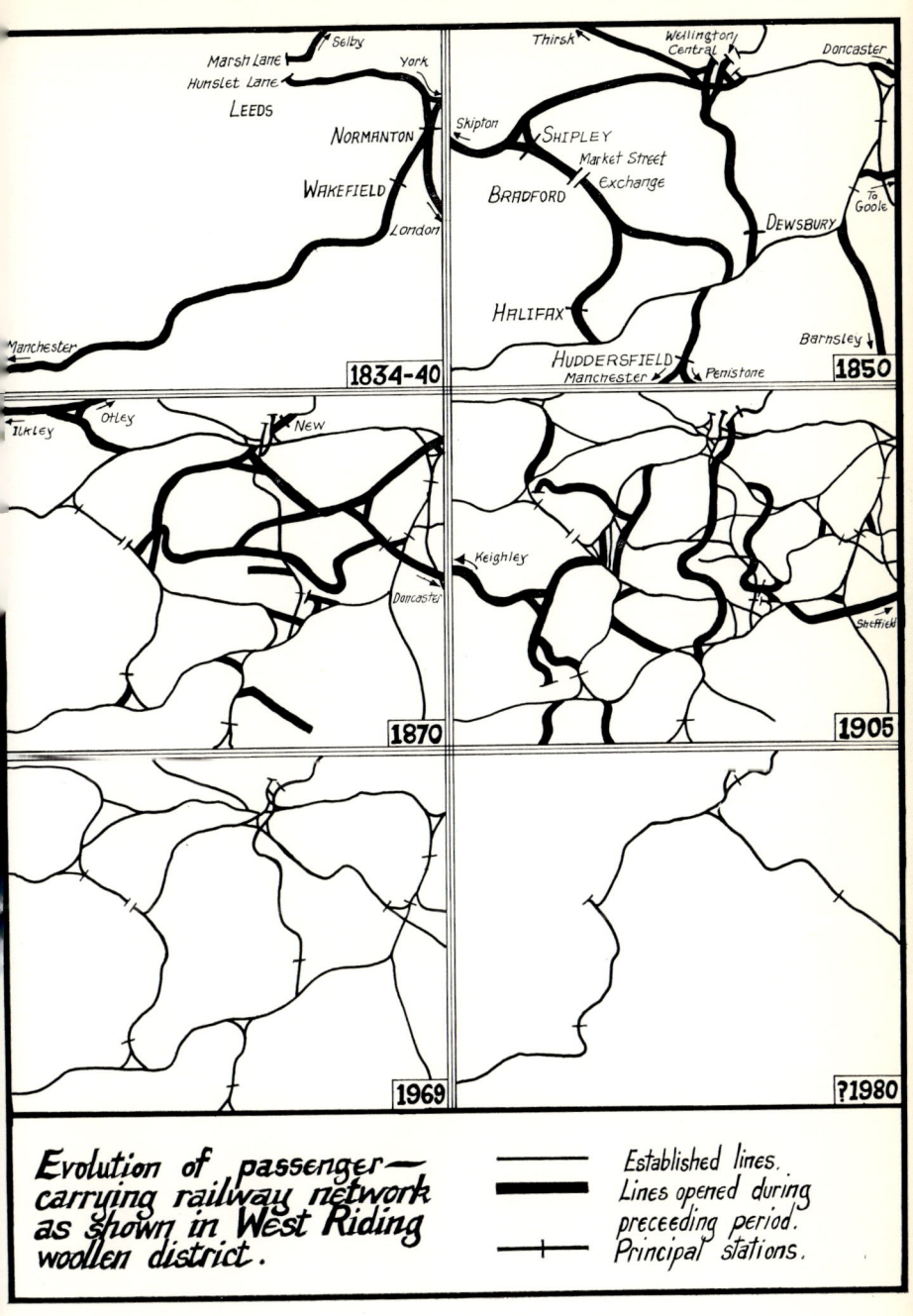

1834-40

Selby
Marsh Lane
Hunslet Lane
LEEDS
York
Normanton
Wakefield
London
Manchester

1850

Thirsk
Wellington Central
Doncaster
Skipton
SHIPLEY
Market Street Exchange
BRADFORD
DEWSBURY
To Goole
HALIFAX
Barnsley
HUDDERSFIELD
Manchester
Penistone

1870

Otley
Ilkley
New
Keighley
Doncaster

1905

Sheffield

1969

?1980

Evolution of passenger-carrying railway network as shown in West Riding woollen district.

— Established lines.
━ Lines opened during preceeding period.
┼ Principal stations.

Leeds as a railway centre. Five major railways now served the city—the Midland, the North Eastern, the London & North-Western, the Great Northern and the Lancashire & Yorkshire. In the 1860s the North Eastern and the London & North-Western joined forces to build New station adjacent to the existing Midland-owned Wellington station, thus facilitating through journeys across the city. Wellington and New stations were ultimately combined to become the City station, which has handled all Leeds traffic since 1967. The London & North-Western reached Leeds by absorbing the Leeds, Dewsbury & Manchester Railway and the Huddersfield & Manchester Railway, a fine neo-classical style station being built on the route at Huddersfield. Meantime the Great Northern Railway had begun to use the recently closed and little lamented Central station, and was soon operating London expresses as well as a network of local services in the Leeds-Bradford area. The company has long since vanished, but the *Great Northern Hotel* still survives opposite the demolished railway station it was built to serve.

Bradford at this time was served by the Midland at Market Street, later known as Forster Square station, and up to 1967 the Midland-route trains to Sheffield, Derby and St. Pancras departed from this station. The Great Northern and the Lancashire & Yorkshire railways shared Exchange station from 1867, the Great Northern running London expresses while the L & Y operated services to Liverpool and Manchester as well as Halifax and Huddersfield. At one time the Midland had ambitions to build a new route directly across Bradford, and although the land was acquired and remained in railway hands until comparatively recent times, the line was never built. The Great Northern did however connect Shipley with their network by a steep branch via Thackley.

Sheffield was very much the heart of Midland territory, served by what became the main Midland artery between London and the North and later by the Hope Valley line through the Peak District to Manchester. It was also connected with Manchester by the Manchester, Sheffield & Lincolnshire railway through Woodhead. The old Woodhead tunnel had the reputation of being the most murderous tunnel ever constructed; hundreds of men lost their lives through accidents and as a result of outbreaks of cholera in the squalid little shanty towns in which they lived. There was an enquiry and a national scandal over the number of deaths. The route later became part of the Great Central Railway, the last main line to reach London, and was electrified between Sheffield and

Manchester after the Second World War.

The port of Hull was well served by the powerful North Eastern Railway, but the rival Hull & Barnsley Railway was opened in 1885 to try and break the North Eastern monopoly. The attempt did not succeed and the line, one of the last major routes built in Yorkshire, eventually passed into North Eastern hands. By the 1880s the railway network of the county was not only virtually complete, but was much larger and more comprehensive than at present. The rich and powerful companies continued to extend their empires, sometimes needlessly duplicating routes and rivalling each other in the speed and excellence of their finest services. That now almost vanished part of the English landscape, the rural branch line came into being.

The North Eastern, which by 1872 had built that splendid tribute to the Age of Iron, York Station, soon developed a very comprehensive network of such lines in North Yorkshire. Initially there was great interest in the Cleveland Hills as a source of iron ore for the growing steel industry of Middlesbrough. The long-vanished Rosedale railway was built for this purpose, and had a stationary engine above Battersby to haul lines of mineral wagons up to the high plateau of the North York Moors. Part of the line now forms a section of the Lyke Wake Walk. Many other branches were developed, linking villages such as Helmsley, Coxwold and Kirkbymoorside with Pickering, Malton and Scarborough. A much lamented route was the coastal line from Saltburn and Redcar over Staithes viaduct to Whitby and then on to Scarborough. The sole survivor in the area is the single track Whitby-Middlesbrough line, winding down Eskdale and serving villages like Egton, Glaisdale and Danby where the roads are too steep to permit buses to operate. But most of the branch lines have vanished, some in the recent and some in the remoter past.

In the West Riding, with its larger population, the competition was to secure the highly profitable urban routes. The suburbs themselves were a creation of Victorian rail and tramway systems, which enabled middle-class people to live in pleasant places well away from their work. Towns and villages like Ilkley, Harrogate, Menston, Otley and Wetherby all developed with amazing speed in the railway age. Lines of comfortable well-built villas of the 1880s and 1890s testify to the power of the railway to change the landscape.

There was a fair amount of rivalry for the lucrative Wharfedale traffic. The Midland opened a spur from its main line from Leeds to Guiseley and Burley, and later developed a corresponding route from Bradford. The town of Otley was soon reached by a North Eastern spur from Arthington, and the Midland and North Eastern built a joint line from Otley to Burley and Ilkley. Through Harrogate-Bradford and Ilkley-Harrogate services were operated. I remember Otley station in its last days with the massive buildings constructed for the busy hoards of commuters of the 1890s looking distinctly ghost-like. The rails were already beginning to rust, and the trains—two per day—carried only a pathetic handful of passengers. Only a few years previously the line had still been a popular outlet to the Yorkshire Dales. The route between Ilkley and Skipton was opened in 1888, and this enabled through excursion trains to be run from the big cities to Bolton Abbey—a facility that continued until the last days of the line.

Another outlet for town dwellers to reach the country was provided by the Nidderdale line between Harrogate and Pateley Bridge which was opened in 1862 and continued in use for passengers until 1951. Rail facilities were extended when Bradford Corporation constructed a light railway, originally for carting materials and workers to its Angram and Scar House reservoirs, but later kept open for villagers and tourists. It was once possible to have a day's rail excursion from Leeds or Bradford right up to Lofthouse near the head of the dale. The line was closed in 1936, but its permanent way now makes a fascinating raised footway along the valley bottom. The old station at Lofthouse is now a cottage that serves teas, and in the original booking hall the ticket window is still to be seen.

The Yorkshire Dales Railway between Skipton and Grassington, opened in 1902, remains in use to convey lime-stone from the lime works at Swinden, and very occasionally ramblers excursion trains have been run along it. Railways in remoter parts of the Dales were not always welcomed with enthusiasm. There was a great deal of anger and concern when plans were announced to build a railway through Grassington and Kettlewell to join the line between Leyburn and Hawes at Aysgarth. This presumably would have necessitated a tunnel under the shoulder of Buckden Pike, but what really enraged country lovers was the prospect of a huge iron bridge over Aysgarth Falls. John Ruskin and William Morris were among the angry protesters at this intended intrusion of industrialism in one of the loveliest places in Wensleydale. It is an odd quirk of fate that whereas country lovers of the 19th century furiously defended their precious heritage against the coming of railways, those of the 20th century fight with equal zeal to keep the lines open. Perhaps the 20th century alternative—the motor car—is in many people's eyes far worse. Certainly Ruskin and Morris had a point; the scheme was in any event financially unsound and nothing came of it.

Apart from the many other profound and complex effects the coming of the railways had on our society, including it is said the formation of the Trade Union movement, there were deep and lasting changes in the countryside and the towns. Railways enabled towns to spread out into the country; the town was like an octopus and the railway its tentacle. Folk from remote villages in the Dales or Wolds, attracted by the wealth and excitement of the towns, were often eager to migrate and work among urban surroundings, thus accelerating the process of depopulation of rural areas. Inhabitants of the big cities of Leeds, Sheffield, Bradford, Middlesbrough and Hull saw the beauty which was near to them and contrasted so violently with the squalor of the towns. The outdoor movement was born.

In terms of traffic and route mileage, railways reached their peak in the years just before the First War. The Victorian railway system was in many respects superb. It was possible to reach almost any part of the county by rail and, although remote branch lines might be operated by decrepit engines and stock, the best trains compared very favourably indeed with the present day and were usually more frequent. Average speeds in the 1880s were about 40 to 50 m.p.h. on main line expresses and on branch lines about 20 to 30 m.p.h, rather better than present day rural buses. The steam engine was a way of life; the plume of smoke on the horizon and the faint whistle of a distant locomotive was part of the natural order of things, like sunrise or sunset.

Perhaps one can be forgiven for nostalgia. The steam engine was more than just a source of power; it was a symbol of Britain's 19th century greatness and supremacy as an industrial nation. Locomotives were not just utilitarian machines, but living creations of iron and steel, things of beauty stamped with the designer's individuality and the tradition within which he worked. Doubts on this score can be answered by visiting the Railway Museum at York and seeing the splendid North Eastern engines kept there; the last designs were the culmination of 200 years' concentrated engineering sophistication and know-how. But even before the First War forces were at work to destroy the age of steam. Technological and social changes, accelerated by two major wars, soon exploded the Edwardian myth of supremacy. Is it too fanciful to suggest

The two futures of rural railways? Above: Voluntary support by a preservation society as shown by this works train on the section of the Whitby-Pickering railway which may soon be re-opened between Grosmont and Eller Beck (John M. Boyes). Below: Adaptation into a footpath as at Sandsend (Tony Edenbrow).

that the last steam engines in Yorkshire seemed in a peculiar way to carry with them an especial melancholia? How vividly one remembers the last grubby but undefeated "Black Fives" or "Evening Star" classes on the Settle-Carlisle, all steam and glory, trailing a long line of empty mineral wagons over Ribblehead viaduct with the sun just vanishing behind the black ridge of Whernside.

There are plenty of remnants. The Whitby-Middlesbrough line with its stations and signalling equipment is, apart from modern diesel cars, a living survival of a Victorian rural railway. Country stations that are in use are still almost exactly as they were in the 1870s or 1880s, with gas or even oil lamps, station furniture and buildings remaining much as they were. There is plenty for the railway archaeologist to discover and explore in Yorkshire. Ordnance maps show the tell-tale "track of old railway" with its embankments and cuttings, although bridges have usually been demolished. A route one once knew well is quickly reduced to a broad grassy path, the lines being ripped up and equipment demolished with an energy which contrasts surprisingly with a century's lethargy in operating the line. Abandoned railways could make fascinating walks, away from the noise and bustle of roads. The old Nidderdale railway was on the point of being bought by the county council as a foot and bridle path but the money was not available and the opportunity was lost. It is a beautiful route.

Railway technology, and in particular steam technology, is being kept alive by several enthusiastic societies in the county. The Middleton Railway Trust has acquired the historic Middleton line and now operates commercial services with steam and diesel engines, while most railway enthusiasts in Yorkshire are sooner or later likely to find their way to Haworth where the Keighley and Worth Valley Railway Preservation Society has bought the Keighley-Oxenhope line. Regular week-end services are run using part of the extensive collection of steam locomotives. The North Yorkshire Moors Railway Preservation Society is negotiating with British Rail, and hopes soon to operate services on the historic Whitby-Pickering line, while the Yorkshire Dales Railway Society plans to establish a transport museum at Embsay station and possibly run services on the Skipton-Grassington line. It is railway mania all over again, but if some of these enthusiastic groups manage to retain something of the magic and beauty of the age of steam they will be doing later generations a very great service.

9: Return to the Roads

WITH the coming of the railways coaching suffered a dramatic decline. Trains were faster and cheaper, and the once-crowded roads and inns soon became relatively deserted. Stage-coach owners and inn-keepers, if they were wise, bought shares in the new railway companies. Times were harsh for coachmen, for servants at the now half-empty inns and for toll-keepers whose incomes dwindled away almost to nothing. It would be wrong to assume that traffic entirely vanished from the roads in the railway age for there were plenty of places where railways never penetrated and local stage-coach or wagonette services remained in use. In the 1850s prior to the building of the Nidd Valley railway a horse omnibus, timed to meet trains coming to and from Harrogate and Ripon, was run between Nidd Bridge station and Pateley Bridge. There was also a fair amount of local commercial traffic on Yorkshire's roads and lanes—farm carts, hay wains and local deliveries made by the village carter who would often run a wagonette service to cater for remote places. Victorian gentry of any status kept their own carriages and stable of horses, and in most country towns post-chaises were available for hire.

The loss of through traffic caused the turnpike managers much anxiety, and also worried the government. As there were hardly sufficient tolls to pay the toll-keepers' wages, there was nothing left to repair the roads which seemed likely to deteriorate to their pre-turnpike state. The 1835 Highways Act had put all non-turnpike roads on to the parish rates, while Acts passed in the 1860s largely resolved the difficulty. These gave powers to local authorities to repair certain turnpikes, and in 1871 an Act was passed which abolished turnpikes and made local authorities responsible for the repair of all roads.

In Yorkshire's towns and cities the problem was different. Roads were traditionally made and repaired by the city authorities, and as far as transport was concerned the suburban railways—mainly developed in the 1860s and '70s—provided an excellent network of services to and from the urban centres. But they could not penetrate into the heart of a city, and horse omnibuses were soon being operated for the benefit of those too poor to own a carriage or hire a cab.

These were usually small single-decker vehicles, although sometimes double-decker, which must have been difficult to control or manage through a crowded and cobbled street. The answer was quite simple—to put the bus on rails which would give a smoother passage and allow far larger loads to be hauled. Horse tramways were soon being built all over the country, and were given greater impetus by the government when the Tramway Act was passed in 1870. The following year Leeds had its first horse tram service operated by the Leeds Tramway Company out to Headingley on what significantly is still bus route No. 1. Services in other Yorkshire cities soon followed.

It might be asked why horses were used in an age of such great mechanisation. In fact experiments had been made with steam carriages as early as 1830, when one capable of carrying ten people at a speed of 10 m p.h. on the level and 6 m.p.h. up hill was constructed in Huddersfield. The enormous size and weight of the vehicle, the noise and the steam, smoke and even hot coals emitted would have been all very well if the vehicle had been on the secluded tracks of a railway, but were not appreciated on city streets. The damage to road surfaces and the risk of scaring horses were particularly resented, and the reaction of turnpike trustees was to raise tolls to £3 per vehicle which effectively froze development. In the 1870s steam had become more socially acceptable, in spite of the punitive "Red Flag" Acts of 1861 and 1865 designed to prevent the development of mechanised road vehicles. By 1879 the Board of Trade had relented sufficiently to allow steam traction on roads, providing there was no smoke and speed was restricted to 10 m.p.h. This presented quite a problem for would-be designers of steam trams, and elaborate contraptions were invented to condense the steam and at least reduce the smoke. Leeds, so often a transport pioneer, experimented with a locally-made Kitson steam tram in 1877, but it was in Huddersfield—the first municipality to build and operate its own tramway system—that steam had a fair degree of success. The system, which extended as far as Marsden by 1911, was 4ft. 7¾ins. gauge and carried a great deal of freight, especially coal, thus rivalling the railway. Steam trams in the centre of Huddersfield must have been quite a sight, "snorting and rocking along the tracks, emitting sulphurous fumes and vapours from their chimneys" while climbing up some steep Pennine bank. There was a particularly nasty accident in 1883 when one ran out of control, and they were occasionally known

to explode. The Huddersfield system served the community in
a variety of ways—there was a local parcels service, refuse
wagon service and the first "letter box on trams" scheme. Perhaps the most attractive touch of all was a delivery service
whereby a wife, for only 3d per week, could put a hot dinner-
can on a tram-car and have it delivered at her husband's factory.

It was the Leeds Tramway Company, realising the dis-
advantages of steam power for the relatively light loads and
short movements of street-cars, which experimented very
successfully with electric traction in 1891 by the conversion
of the Harehills-Roundhay line. Leeds thus had the first

70

The tramway age. Opposite page:-Top: Left: Early electric car at Thornhill about 1905 (collection of J. Taylor). Right: Twilight of the Leeds tramway system in 1959 (David Joy). Centre: First electric tramcar at Summit on August 10th, 1905 (collection of R. Wilkinson). Bottom: Scarborough tramways showing (left) a runaway into a ballroom (both collection of R. Wardill). This page: Steam tram in Bingley Road, Saltaire (loaned by R. Pouncey).

electric tramway system in Yorkshire, an important innovation being the use of overhead pick-up wires. The tram terminus—now a car park—is still clearly visible by the side of Roundhay Park. Bradford too, faced with an extremely hilly town centre, soon experimented with electric traction, and in 1892 was using cars with an extremely advanced gearing system. Yorkshire's tramways developed quickly in the years prior to the First World War. Sheffield soon had one of the finest systems in England, and Hull, Scarborough, Halifax, Keighley, York and Rotherham all had tramway networks. It was possible, albeit with frequent changes and the occasional walk of a mile or two, to cross the Pennines from Leeds to Liverpool by tramcar in a day by leaving at dawn and arriving almost at dusk. In certain areas trams rivalled the rail service—for instance between Guiseley and Leeds—and if slower they were at least cheaper. One misfortune of the Yorkshire system was the variety of gauges. Halifax had a narrow 3ft. 6ins. gauge for the very hilly terrain—at the highest point the cars climbed to over 1,000ft. and thus surely achieved a record for this country. Bradford had a 4ft. gauge and Leeds the standard

71

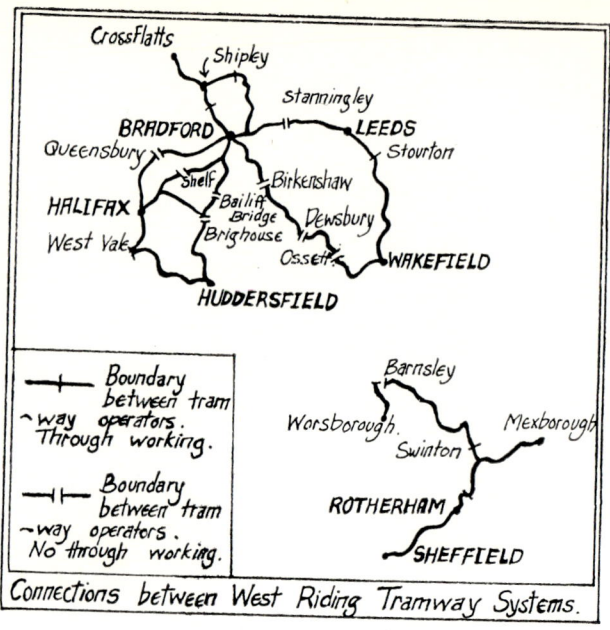

Connections between West Riding Tramway Systems.

4ft. 8½ins. Through trips between the two cities were thus impossible, experimental cars with movable wheels not being a great success.

Following the Light Railways Act of 1896 tramway systems had further scope to develop. Briefly a light railway is a simplified railway, lighter in construction than a conventional line and not subject to such strict safety precautions because of lower speeds. This enabled municipal authorities to build and operate lines more cheaply than previously—Bradford Corporation's upper Nidderdale line has already been cited. The only true example of a surviving light railway is the privately owned Derwent Valley line built to serve rural areas south of York. Although much of the line is closed, it still manages to operate a freight service between York and the village of Elvington seven miles away. More significantly the light railway principle was soon adapted to tramway systems, and undertakings laid tracks across open country, by the sides of roads, or sometimes—as between Bradford and Huddersfield—on a reserved central track. The advantages of a reserved track were considerable, tramcars being able to make swift progress unimpeded by other traffic. In Leeds there were fine reserved tracks between York Road and Temple Newsam, while the city built a full light railway for its trams through to Middleton. These reserved strips, now usually grassed over, remain as areas of green along the edges of crowded roads.

But increasingly there was a move away from the restriction of rails back to the freedom of the road. Steam traction finally came into its own in the late 19th and early 20th centuries with the development of traction engines, those powerful and adaptable machines which for 50 years were supreme in all tasks of heavy haulage on roads in town and country. John Fowler Ltd. of Leeds produced justly famous machines which could haul incredibly huge loads. They were adaptable to a number of roles—tractors, haulage units, suppliers of power (particularly noteworthy on fairgrounds) and the ubiquitous steam rollers which have only very recently vanished from Yorkshire's roads.

It was human muscle power as well as steam power which heralded the return to the roads. The growing populations of towns and cities in the West Riding were soon able to reach the countryside on the bicycle, a remarkably efficient and inexpensive invention. In the 1880s and '90s the sport of cycling became fashionable for young and old, in spite of rough roads and primitive machines, and the once deserted inns were suddenly filled again with clubs of hungry and thirsty cyclists. Cycling however is for the energetic; particularly on Dales roads it can be immensley hard work. Something was needed which gave mobility without the effort, and it came in the form of the internal combustion engine.

The invention of the petrol engine is usually attributed to a German engineer, Dr. Otto. The principle is not dissimilar to that of the steam engine but using an explosive mixture of petrol and air electrically ignited. It is not surprising to discover that the builders of many great motor cars—for example W. H. Bentley—were apprenticed in railway engineering. Certainly one can see the evolution of the internal combustion engine as a development of many of the most sophisticated techniques of steam engineering, requiring the same degree of precision workmanship. As with the canal age, the steam age made possible the next age—the car age. The first horseless carriages were crude, even slightly comic creations, compared with the smooth perfection of the steam engines of the 1890s. The frail carriage body on rubber-tyred coach wheels with a pathetic little stuttering engine must have made the directors of the great railway companies smile. But the smile was soon wiped off their faces.

By 1896 British Daimler was established, and designs improved with incredible speed. The "Red Flag" law was repealed and this was the beginning of extraordinary progress. In the U.S.A. Henry Ford was soon to design his model "T" opening the way for mass production. Motor lorries, crude and unreliable though they were, soon made their appearance, while experiments were made with motor buses and charabancs. The early attempts were disappointing; a vehicle in daily service needs to be tougher than most but just before the outbreak of the war London General were operating their reliable type-B bus. The First World War was important to transport in two ways. Firstly the railways—taken over by the Government—were operated as a national system for the first time, but they also received terrific wear and tear as the nation's over-worked arteries. Secondly it was the first truly mechanised war, requiring not cavalry but tanks, tough transport vehicles, lorries and aircraft. The London type-B bus excelled itself as a troop carrier in impossible conditions, and thus became a prototype for future designs.

In 1919 the Ministry of Transport was set up to sort out the chaos of the war-scarred railways and co-ordinate the nation's transport affairs. It was debated whether to nationalise but eventually it was decided to form four gigantic companies—the Great Western Railway, Southern Railway, London Midland and Scottish Railway, and London and North Eastern Railway. Yorkshire's principal railways were thus split between the L.M.S. (the Midland, the London & North-Western, and the Lancashire & Yorkshire) and the L.N.E.R. (the Great Northern, Great Central, North Eastern, and Hull & Barnsley). The aim was to create a bigger, more efficient and truly national network, and in many ways this was achieved. But it could not stem the inevitable tide. Passengers and freight slowly drifted away while profits declined. What were the reasons for this? Partially it was the railways' own fault—the glorious days of Victorian monopoly had made them complacent and practices and methods which suited the companies rather than the customer remained unchanged. The remote London headquarters were inflexible in ideas of operation. Many branch lines, built more in hope than careful commercial evaluation, continued in operation long after they should have been closed—the companies hung on to their empires as long as possible. There was insufficient capital available to modernise, particularly in the provincial areas which included Yorkshire, and it was basically the old

Victorian system—in some cases with the very same loco-motives and rolling stock let alone stations—that wheezed on until the middle of the 20th century.

The other reason of course was the development of rival systems. After the First War ex-army lorries could be obtained cheaply, and people used war benefits or savings to buy an old lorry. A local carrier who had survived the lean times with a couple of wagons would acquire a lorry, then perhaps a charabanc. Prices would be cheaper, the service tailored to people's needs, and thus trade would grow, slowly eroding the railway monopoly. The increasing number of road licences issued in the years before the Second World War indicates the growth of the road transport industry. In 1904 the figure was 4,000 which rose to 82,000 in 1914, 173,000 in 1923 and almost 500,000 in 1938. Similarly with passenger transport the number of buses on the road operated by private companies as well as municipalities grew rapidly. Prosperous firms quickly bought out their rivals, or were formed as a result of several smaller companies amalgamating. The West Yorkshire Road Car Company, for example, began as a small Harrogate firm which soon expanded to cover a huge area of Yorkshire, even taking over Keighley Corporation services in 1932. United, which now covers the whole of North Yorkshire, has over 100 small companies and undertakings incorporated into it. Sheffield Corporation, as well as operating one of the most extensive tramway systems in England, also extended their motor bus operations well into the countryside around the city, taking in much of the Peak District.

Although the larger companies began steadily to extend their empires in the 1920s and '30s, there was a fair amount of trouble when small operators—sometimes not even working to a regular timetable—"pirated" passengers from the big operators by running buses just a few minutes ahead of their rivals, thus sweeping up the cream of the traffic. This kind of ruthless and unfair competition had to be prevented, so in 1930 the Road Traffic Act was passed establishing Traffic Commissioners for road passenger services over the entire country. Their function was to examine the road transport needs of a given area and alocate licences only to operators who were capable of providing a good and reliable service The licence gave a company monopoly over a specified route, but in return for this an adequate service had to be maintained. Since 1930 therefore big companies with huge staffs and plenty of well-maintained vehicles have gradually come to

Town and country buses. Above: "Pioneer" operating an early urban service between Colne and Earby. Left: A "Bounty" bus at Whitewell on the run from Slaidburn to Clitheroe typifies the independent rural service .

dominate services in the Yorkshire traffic area, and as small companies have found themselves in economic difficulties they have been taken over by their wealthier rivals. Recent examples have been the acquisition of Samuel Ledgards by West Yorkshire, and the control of Pennine Motors by Ribble. The inter-urban and country services in Yorkshire are now operated by Ribble Motors (the extreme west of the county), West Yorkshire, United, East Yorkshire (who possess a fleet of unique domed-roof buses designed to fit under the low gateway of Beverley Bar) and, in the mining and heavy woollen areas, the Yorkshire Woollen and West Riding with Hanson serving the Huddersfield district.

But the small operators have not entirely vanished. There were many routes spurned by the big companies as being quite unlucrative, which a small man—perhaps a garage owner or village joiner—could just make pay. Sometimes these local men were survivors of the railway age and had managed to operate a one or two horse wagonette before saving up to buy a second-hand bus. An owner-conductor-driver—perhaps helped out by a friend on market day—could run a service and make a slight profit where the big company would fail. There is a peculiar pleasure about travelling on a little country bus such as the Reliance coach from York to Crayke, the Hillcrest bus from Settle to Horton, or Percivals splendid old "flyers" that run up Swaledale as far as Gunnerside, Keld and Arkengarthdale. Even some of the big companies' rural services have their own special charm—for instance the United buses which run up Wensleydale or the West Yorkshire route to Lofthouse in Nidderdale. The drivers are invariably wits with a fund of tales and comment. A bus will suddenly grind to a halt in the middle of a village or by a lonely crossroads with the engine ticking over for a good two minutes until old Mrs. Smith appears with her market basket or comes to collect a parcel sent from the town. A country bus is a meeting place, somewhere to gossip and hear the latest news. Time doesn't seem to matter quite as much, although I well remember a driver—annoyed because an old dear invariably arrived at the cross-roads three minutes late—announcing one day that he would wait no longer and the four hour gap until the next bus would surely cure her. The motorist speeding down the dale misses a great deal of the true dales life.

Buses may be slow, but they are convenient. In the main operators have managed to run a more frequent service than the railways, and through being able to stop anywhere along the route serve the needs of more people. Faced with the choice of a walk of a mile or two to the nearest station, or a local bus which although slower in making the journey as a whole leaves from the lane end, country people have invariably opted for buses. The Nidd Valley branch line closed in 1951 because of the success of a rival bus service. The buses of 1969 take a third as long again as the trains did in 1869, but the buses are still running while the railway has vanished.

The cheapness, flexibility and convenience of road buses soon affected city tramway systems just as much as the railways. Many have questioned the wisdom of this development for up-to-date tramways and light railways have proved immensely popular and efficient in almost every country in Western Europe except our own. The British, an island people to the last, are unique in believing (at least in Yorkshire) that road passenger transport in cities can fulfil our needs. Admittedly the ancient tramcars rolling along tracks situated in the centre of busy urban roads and streets were an anachronism, but a modern rapid transit system sited underground, overhead or on reserved tracks would be a different proposition. Unfortunately it was decided to demolish rather than modernise, and even Leeds and Sheffield—possessing extensive and relatively up-to-date systems—were abandoned with remarkable speed in

77

the 1950s. The last Leeds tram ran in November 1959, while the last tram in Yorkshire ran in Sheffield on October 8th, 1960.

For a nation that removed its tramways so ruthlessly and rapidly, we have an odd nostalgia for the tram. They really were rather impressive vehicles — big, noisy, ugly, but immensely efficient movers of crowds. They were uncomfortable but somehow friendly and dignified, clattering and banging over points. There are some Leeds and Sheffield tramcars at Crich Tramway Museum near Matlock, Derbyshire, and I believe Bradford Corporation is secretly very proud of one it has hidden away somewhere which is occasionally allowed to exercise on a few yards of concealed track like a grand old lady being permitted to stroll out on to her balcony. Trolley-buses—originally designed to augment and sometimes repalce tramway services—have had a similar fate. The only city in Yorkshire really to go in for them in a big way was Bradford, and although silent, efficient and cheap to operate they too have succumbed to the diesel engine. The last trolleybuses will soon be leaving the few routes they still operate in Bradford, and then Middlesbrough will be the only town in England retaining this type of vehicle.

The most significant rival to the railways and later to the road passenger operators has of course been the private car. Henry Ford designed his model "T" in 1909; it was intended to be a "people's car" but mass motoring really began after the Great War. At the motor show at Olympia in 1922 Sir Herbert Austin's ugly little Austin 7 was displayed, costing £225. By the end of that year the car with a larger engine was selling for £165. Cheap motoring was coming. But the process was delayed in the 1920s and '30s by the Great Strike and the Depression. During the Second World War motoring was almost impossible, and even for a few years afterwards cars were difficult to obtain and expensive. In fact public transport —both road and rail—had a minor boom in the late 1940s and early '50s, bus travel especially reaching a peak about 1950 from which it has rapidly declined. From the middle '50s onwards wages started to rise, goods were again obtainable, the word "affluence" began to be curent. Cheap and highly successful cars were on the market—the Morris 1000 which sold a million in a few years, Ford Anglias, Populars, A40s, and then the familiar Minis, Vivas, Volkswagens, Fiats and Renaults. Motoring was no longer the exclusive pastime of the rich; it was suddenly within the means of most people. The implications of this simple fact are enormous.

10: The Car Age

A car is go where you want. A car is the whole family together cheaply and conveniently. A car is a little home on
wheels. A car is freedom. But when 12, 20 or even 30 million
other people have that freedom, and all want to exercise it in
similar places at a similar time, the result is a complete loss of
all freedom. It is a nightmare. Car ownership is growing at a
fantastic speed. In 1939 there were over two million cars on the
road. By 1959 this had more than doubled. But in only eight
years—from 1959 to 1967—this figure more than doubled
again to over ten million. The Ministry of Transport's own
official calculations suggest an even more dramatic increase.
By 1970 there will be over 12 million cars, by 1980 21 million,
by 1990 26 million, by 2000 31 million, and by 2010—saturation
—35 million! These are only estimates, but evidence suggests
that Yorkshire has less cars than the national average and can
be expected to catch up. Young people now growing up will
expect to own and use a car as a matter of right, unlike many
middle-aged people who have never taken a driving test and
understandably are now too nervous to drive. So high on young
people's priorities is a car that many couples will often buy one
before getting a house.

This increase in car ownership—or something very like it—
will certainly come, and the effects of it on every aspect of our
daily life are too obvious to need description. But the present
transport revolution—perhaps the most profound and far-
reaching that has ever happened—has disturbing consequences
for Yorkshire and its inhabitants. Public transport is now
being severely hit by the growth of car ownership, and the
familiar vicious spiral has been created. Imagine a Dales village
served —as many were until quite recently—by a rail and bus
route. Suppose the train needs an average load of 30 passengers
to make it pay and the bus about 20 with the routes being just
self-supporting. Then five people in the village buy a car, and
perhaps take a friend to work or to the nearby town. The railway managers soon notice that traffic has fallen slightly and
decide they must try and save money, which they do by reducing

the service. This so annoys and inconveniences five more people in the village that they decide to buy a car; the railway managers therefore cut the service even more. Soon where there were 30 passengers there are now five, and trains are reduced to one or two a day. Then the line is closed as costs of keeping a near-deserted railway open are almost those of maintaining quite a busy line. The few remaining passengers travel for a short time on the slower bus, but because the bus has raised fares to make up for its lost passengers they soon save up for their own transport and, as is happening increasingly all over Yorkshire, the bus services are reduced in frequency.

This process was accelerated in 1963 with the publication of the Beeching Report, which gave renewed impetus to the rationalisation of rail services. Since that time the wholesale closure of the Yorkshire rail network has proceeded piecemeal, sometimes clumsily and crudely with little real awareness of the complex social and economic consequences that would ensue. Already over half the routes in Yorkshire—including several important main lines—have been closed, and it is probable that many more will go in the near future leaving the county with a skeleton rail service comprising the London routes, perhaps one cross-Pennine line and little else. This contrasts rather savagely with the extensive modernisation and rebuilding of railways in the London area, where two completely new routes—the Victoria and Fleet lines of the Underground—are also being constructed.

Clearly it was only good sense to close little used lines in remote rural backwaters. But many axed lines were extremely busy—for instance the important suburban service between Bradford Forster Square and Leeds was closed in 1965. even though at peak times passengers were standing in the crowded trains. Cononley station near Skipton served the centre of the village and was even making a profit, but services were still removed. Even the main Sheffield-Leeds-Scotland line, the old Midland route, is now threatened, while such important resorts as Bridlington and Filey have had to fight for their essential rail links. There is little evidence of any real planning from Whitehall, and railway administrators are clearly quite out of touch with local needs. Only recently it was decided to retain the line between Skipton and Colne as Skipton's main outlet to the south, while Leeds-Skipton line was to be closed. A year later the decision was reversed; the Colne line is now to be closed and the Leeds line will perhaps remain open. Some Yorkshire services have been retained by means of "social grants" under the terms of the 1968 Transport Act, but these are only temporary and are subject to the whims of politicians wondering how they can save taxpayers' money without causing more than a local outcry. Some development has occurred in recent years on Yorkshire's rail system, notably the rebuilding of Leeds City station, the establishment of the central administrative offices of the Eastern Region at York, the introduction of a few high speed diesel trains to the south and the creation of Freightliner services from many important centres. But the overall prospect remains gloomy. Competition from motorways will make further inroads into rail traffic, and unless there is some radical managerial rethinking the railways of Yorkshire may have almost vanished by the late 1970s.

Bus services have fared little better. Initially they benefited from the decline of the railways, but are now subject to the same pressures. As car ownership increases, and as fares rise, so passengers decline and the services are curtailed. In the Yorkshire area alone in 1966-7 no less than 16 bus services were reduced in frequency or completely suspended, and by 1967-8 this figure had risen to nineteen. Tiny operators running a single service once a week—or perhaps even once a month— to the local market are having to abandon their routes. The larger companies have up to now managed to keep most of their services running by single-man operation and a policy of "cross-subsidisation"—the subsidising of loss-making country buses by the profits made on busy inter-urban services. But as the growth of car ownership eats into the usage of the busy routes their profitability is reduced, and it is only a matter of time before there will not be enough money to finance the country routes

David St. John Thomas, in his researches published in *The Rural Transport Problem* in 1963, has revealed how the poor and elderly—especially womenfolk—suffer when bus and rail services are withdrawn. About half the families in Britain still do not own a car, and in poorer areas including many parts of the North the percentage must be higher. Even when a family does have a car it is likely to be used by the husband in his work; the wife will be isolated from the village shops or relatives in the nearby town, and the daughter may find it difficult to attend night school or get a new job. Friends with cars often give lifts but many people, particularly the elderly, consider that it is humiliating to be always cadging a ride. In a small hamlet not five miles from Northallerton I recently

81

spoke to one old woman who for nearly two years had relied entirely on local deliveries instead of going to town to shop. She used to go frequently when the weekly market bus operated but now, reluctant to beg a ride from neighbours, she would rather stay at home. Another married couple I met recently at Stamford Bridge had recently moved to the East Riding from the south and spoke of the isolation of living in the village without a car. The rail service was withdrawn in 1966, and the bus service is poor. They were determined to acquire a car or leave the area.

The consequences of the continued reduction of public transport from rural areas are all too plain to see. Depopulation will increase for faced with isolation and inconvenience people are going to leave. The *Review of Yorkshire and Humberside* prepared by the Economic Planning Council in 1967 spoke of the problems of communication as being the most vital that threatened Yorkshire's prosperity in the 1970s with the road system being grossly overloaded and the railways seriously underused. Yet decisions of London politicians seem certain to make the situation even worse. It is now quicker to fly to America than to reach some of the not-so-remote parts of the Dales and Wolds by public transport. One only needs to study a railway map of about 1900 or a bus-route map of ten years ago to realise what is happening—and the signs are that there may be many more reductions of service to come.

There is a faint gleam of hope in the 1968 Transport Act which recognises that in the late 20th century public transport can be vitally necessary for a community and yet fail to be self-supporting. Grants have been announced for several rail

"Progress" at Grassington. The attractive cobbled square and its surrounding buildings of half a century ago (opposite page, collection of G. H. Banton) are now obscured by a confusion of parked cars (above, W. R. Mitchell).

services, and money may be made available for the purchase of new buses and the retention of routes. It is intended that Passenger Transport Authorities will be set up in certain areas to co-ordinate and run bus and rail services, although this process has already begun in Yorkshire without Whitehall intervention. Close co-operation occurs between municipal authorities and major companies in organising bus services, and rather more collaboration than in the past between bus and rail operators. Despite this it seems rail closures will continue, and bus services be further reduced in frequency. Transport on Sundays is rapidly becoming a nightmare anywhere off the main road and rail routes. Many areas, particularly the Yorkshire Dales and North York Moors National Parks, which ironically are dedicated to be conserved for public enjoyment, are rapidly becoming inaccessible by any form of public transport any day of the week.

The second and perhaps even more serious consequences of the car revolution in Yorkshire is its effect on environment. Looking first of all at the problem in cities and towns one sees the dilemma which Professor Buchanan, in *Traffic in Towns*, has demonstrated to be facing society. Cities cannot possibly accommodate all the motorists who wish to bring in their vehicles, many of them demanding convenient free parking as if a birthright. To do so would require complete rebuilding from scratch—hopelessly uneconomic and in any case utterly undesirable—or alternatively huge flattened areas would have to be created as gigantic and drab parking lots as in downtown Los Angeles. The other possibility, and surely the only realistic approach, is to limit the use of the motor vehicle. Restrictions—bitterly opposed at first—are reluctantly but gradually being accepted in towns, and motorists are being channelled, cajoled, disciplined and directed by traffic lights, parking meters, one way streets, freeways, box junctions and all the now familiar clutter of the traffic engineering schemes which have appeared. Most civilised people will welcome the recently announced plans to ban all traffic from many of the narrow medieval streets of York, thus saving this great and beautiful city from further damage from the car age and creating quiet pedestrian ways in its centre.

All too often the aim has mistakenly been to keep traffic moving at all costs. The result is the screaming and stinking places we now too often recognise as city streets. Leeds, even though it was studied in the Buchanan report, seems at the present stage of planning to be bearing the brunt of the car age. Traffic indeed moves quickly—except at peak times when it is almost at a standstill—and pedestrians must flee for their lives. To cross City Square to the railway station is a hair-raising experience, while one way streets are race tracks with the roar of engines drowning all conversation. The most disturbing aspect of all this is how pedestrians are subjugated to the needs of motor vehicles, and must scurry across the roads between changing lights. One pities the elderly. To be fair the Leeds scheme is far from finished, and a comprehensive system of traffic-free zones and pedestrian walkways is planned with a lot of traffic diverted to through roads of motorway standard. There are also plans to build segregated lanes for buses, which are now hopelessly traffic-bound at peak times. A few hundred yards of these already exist, but it is hoped that fast and comfortable express buses on traffic-free lanes will tempt motorists away from the increasing fatigue and expense of driving and parking. To create such a system will need an extraordinary amount of rebuilding in the city centre in future years, and one wonders if it would not have been cheaper to maintain some of the railway services to and through the suburbs. Railways contain their own traffic-free lanes to the heart of the city, and commuters on the few surviving lines have increased enormously in the last few years as traffic congestion on the roads has got worse.

Bradford, too, in a zeal of rebuilding has betrayed an odd sense of priorities in constructing pedestrian tunnels with long circuitous routes while motor traffic enjoys the direct route and the daylight. It is little wonder that pedestrians in a hurry skip over the retaining railings. Sheffield and Hull share many of the same problems, and it is quite clear that in these cities the rebuilding and improving of roads will again be constantly outpaced by the increasing number of cars. But the high cost of roads and the damage done to neighbouring homes, shops and amenities will prevent unlimited expansion, and the long term solution is inevitably rationing. Motorists, whether they like it or not, are increasingly going to be discouraged from using their cars in city centres at peak periods, and higher parking costs together with the introduction of road pricing by meters would seem to be deterrents of the future. Crowded traffic conditions and lack of parking space in the big cities has in recent years provided a welcome boost to trade in many of Yorkshire's smaller market towns such as Otley, Ilkley, Skipton, Ripon, Harrogate and Keighley. They have not yet reached the point where parking is impossible, and motorists from nearby areas will go to them on Saturday afternoons rather than struggle into the cities. The stage has been reached where many people from Leeds and Bradford actually prefer to travel 12 or 15 miles to Ilkley or Harrogate rather than go into the city centre.

Outside the towns the most urgent problem is caused by the sheer volume of traffic on the old turnpike and coaching roads, which still form most major roads with slight widenings here and there and the worst corners ironed out. What was excellent for a stage coach is narrow, congested and dangerous for the motor traffic of the 1970s. Motorways—fast and straight purpose-built highways without dangerous bends, gradients or right hand turns—are the ideal solution, and by the construction of dual carriageway most of the Great North Road has now been made to motorway standards as far as Durham. Yorkshire's first pure motorway, the M1 connecting Leeds with London, was completed in 1968. It has greatly reduced journey times, and it seems very likely that coach operators and road haulage firms will again benefit at the expense of the railways. The appallingly slow rail journey between Leeds and Sheffield is already being superseded by motorway bus services, and it is to be hoped that the competition improves the railways' efficiency rather than, as has happened too often in the past, causing them to reduce standards still further.

The railways will have to fight even harder to retain traffic when the M62 is opened. The Trans Pennine Motorway is— at least since the building of the Settle and Carlisle railway— the most dramatic civil engineering project Yorkshire has ever experienced. It will go from west of Manchester to the south of Rochdale and then between Halifax and Huddersfield joining the M1 south of Leeds. The full project, expected to cost at least £40 million, includes the impressive Scammonden reservoir where motorway and dam are combined, while blasting through the Pennine grit is providing some of the most difficult constructional work ever undertaken in Western Europe. M62 promises to be a great and beautiful road. It is desperately needed as any unfortunate motorist who has craw- led along behind some black juggernaut over Blackstone Edge or Standedge will testify, and it will go a long way towards im- proving communications between Yorkshire and Lancashire. The intention is to extend the motorway to Humberside, where it will do much to alleviate the isolation of the city of Hull thrust out on the lonely shores of the Humber. When— as surely must happen—Humberside becomes a vast Euro- pean port and one of the largest industrial centres in Britain, the road will have an even greater importance and become one of the busiest and most important highways in Europe.

What of the Yorkshire countryside in the car age? Already popular spots in the Dales or North York Moors are seething masses of motor vehicles on fine Sundays and bank holidays. Malham, Grassington, Hutton-le-Hole, Goathland or any of a score of beauty spots are soon reduced to crowded car parks with the village cottages or market square lost under the mass of metal and glass. Indiscriminate roadside parking alongside or even on open moorland soon turns a fine land- scape into a cluttered parking lot. The owners are quite often averse to of moving more than a few yards from their vehicles, and will sit complete with folding table and chairs, teapot and transistor radio on the crowded and noisy verge of the road. Others remain inside no matter how fine the weather. Perhaps worst of all are the more discriminating who in trying to "get away from it all" drive their vehicles up quiet side roads or even green lanes (which is illegal) or onto open land so that the area quickly ceases to be a remote and lonely spot. People on foot disappear remarkably easily into the landscape. Even

a hundred people in a quiet valley make relatively little intrusion but a dozen cars with their gleaming metal and chrome
destroy all sense of remoteness and timeless beauty over a
wide area. It is the tragedy of the motor car that motorists
in the mass destroy the very thing they most often seek—the
beauty and quiet of the countryside.

It has been computed that once the present motorway
schemes have been completed the population living within half
an hour's drive of the Yorkshire Dales National Park will be
750,000; within an hour, five million; within $1\frac{1}{2}$ hours, $12\frac{1}{2}$
million; within two hours, 16 million. A survey carried out by

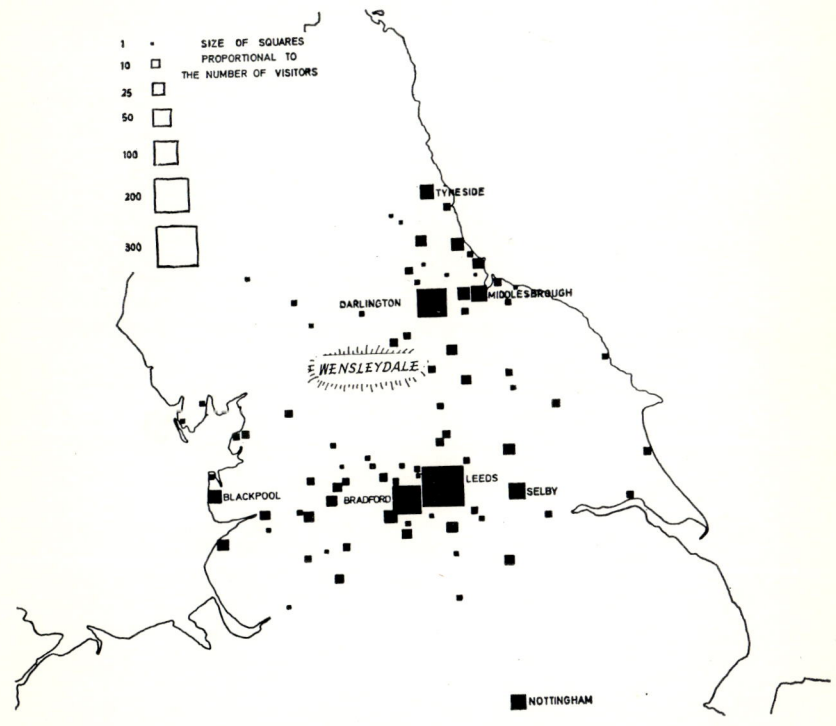

Changes in transport. Above: Visitor pressure on Wensleydale instances the
way in which National Parks are threatened by the mobility of the motor
age. Overleaf: Top: The section of the M62 now under construction north-
west of Huddersfield is perhaps the most dramatic civil engineering project
ever seen in Yorkshire. Bottom: Road improvements which will be needed to
meet expected major expansion on Humberside.

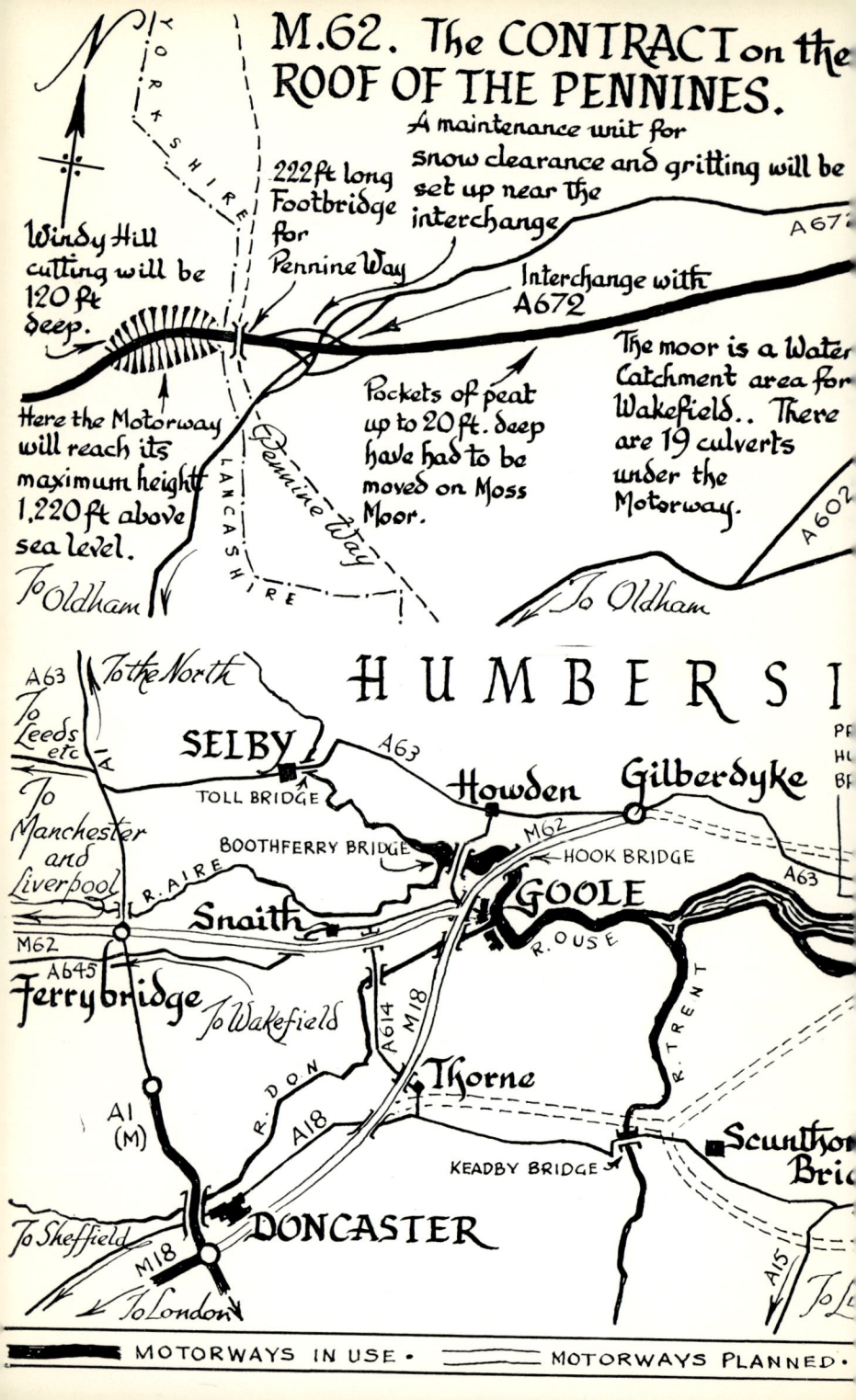

M.62. The CONTRACT on the ROOF OF THE PENNINES.

N

YORKSHIRE

222ft long Footbridge for Pennine Way

A maintenance unit for snow clearance and gritting will be set up near the interchange

A672

Windy Hill cutting will be 120 ft deep.

Interchange with A672

The moor is a Water Catchment area for Wakefield.. There are 19 culverts under the Motorway.

Here the Motorway will reach its maximum height 1,220 ft above sea level.

Pockets of peat up to 20 ft. deep have had to be moved on Moss Moor.

LANCASHIRE

Pennine Way

A602

To Oldham

To Oldham

HUMBERSI

A63

To the North

To Leeds etc

SELBY

A63

TOLL BRIDGE

Howden

Gilberdyke

To Manchester and Liverpool

BOOTHFERRY BRIDGE

M62

HOOK BRIDGE

A63

R. AIRE

Snaith

GOOLE

R. OUSE

M62

A645

Ferrybridge

To Wakefield

A614

M18

R. TRENT

A1 (M)

R. DON

Thorne

A18

Scunthor Bri

KEADBY BRIDGE

To Sheffield

M18

DONCASTER

A15

To L

To London

• MOTORWAYS IN USE • MOTORWAYS PLANNED •

To Halifax

Earth and rock from 150ft deep Deanhead Cut will be used to build Dam.

To Brighouse

Scammonden Dam will be 2,050ft long and 242ft high .... the highest earth-filled dam in Britain

Croft House Cut 90ft deep.

25,000 tons of rock were removed in a single blast

Contractors' Site Office.

To Huddersfield

Scammonden Bridge is to have a single arch of 410ft span — one of the longest in Europe.

A 640

SECTION of DAM

← 180ft →

TOP OF DAM .... 870ft ABOVE SEA LEVEL.

CLAY CORE

MAXIMUM DEPTH OF WATER — 168ft.

FILTERS

CONCRETE GROUT CAP

CLAY & TOP SOIL

SHALE

UPPER KINDERSCOUT GRIT

BLANKET GROUTING

GROUT CURTAIN

1,140 ft

D E

OSED
BER
GE

R. HULL

To Bridlington Filey, and Scarborough

HULL

Hessle

HUMBER FERRY

Hedon

Withernsea

North

Sea

New Holland

HOVERCRAFT SERVICE

PROPOSED HUMBER BARRAGE

Barton upon Humber

Killingholme

A15

IMMINGHAM

SPURN BITE

pe
q

A18

GRIMSBY

Cleethorpes

A18

icoln

To Skegness

To Rotterdam Gothenburg etc.

===== SUGGESTED MOTORWAYS.   ——— PRESENT MAIN ROADS.

the West Riding County Planning Department in July 1967 revealed that between 11.0 a.m. and 8.0 p.m. 22,000 vehicles carrying over 50,000 people entered the National Park. Already many narrow Dales roads are nearing saturation point; on the day of the survey the Ilkley-Bolton Abbey road was carrying 2,983 vehicles while 1,826 cars were on that from Skipton to Grassington. And it is expected that the numbers of people visiting the National Park will increase. There will be great pressure to widen the narrow Dales roads, straightening the characteristic winding lanes and thus attracting even more vehicles. If the needs of the car-owner were to be catered for in the way that many motoring zealots would like to see, the Dales would soon lose their essential character for the narrow lanes—in many cases dating back to monastic times— would be buried under the straight sweep of a dual carriage-way. Would we really value a motorway down Wharfedale or a concrete flyover between Malham and Gordale? Clearly this would never happen, but there is a danger that by piecemeal development—a little widening here and a piece of demolition there—something very like it could come into being.

The situation highlights the dilemma of 20th century man. With all our vast technological know-how we have conquered our environment—the motor car and the aeroplane can cover vast distances with great speed and ease. But we have not learnt to control these machines or to come to terms with them. In the past we were governed by the limitations of our technology; we travelled as fast as the steam engine allowed us and de-velopments automatically constituted progress. Now all has changed and progress is no longer automatic nor inevitable. We must not permit technology to go its own way; it must be steered our way for the future needs to be planned and not just allowed to happen. It will require the most skilled and sensitive planning to achieve the correct course. Scientists are beginning to realise that man sympathetically existing with his own natural background is an essential to human well-being and happiness. The future of the countryside and its careful conservation and management is no mere sentiment-ality or longing for the past but a prime human necessity. National Parks and Areas of Outstanding Natural Beauty have been created to keep as much as possible of Yorkshire's rich rural heritage available for future generations and, even though the ignorant may sometimes deride the planners, the countryside would soon cease to exist without control and re-striction. A shanty town by Bolton Priory or an amusement arcade by Semerwater would be the price of laissez-faire.

So it is in planning for the motor car. There must of course be much more provision for cars and there must be improvement of roads for visitors and residents alike, but it must be done skilfully and discreetly. Car parks must be planned carefully so that they are screened by trees, behind villages or away from viewpoints. Already villages like Buckden and Kettlewell are benefiting from well-sited car parks. More special picnic and play areas with toilets and other amenities for visitors need to be created. Another solution is to develop centres which will give the family motorist what he most wants: a quiet day in the country with something of interest to show the family. Already the Fountains Abbey and Studley Royal estate has been purchased by the West Riding County Council as a Country Park, and is now giving pleasure to many thousands of people as well as preserving a great national monument. Many landowners and owners of fine houses are opening their homes to the public—Castle Howard, Newby Hall, Rudding Park and Nostell Priory are among many which cater for thousands of visitors each summer as well as earning useful sums for the owners.

This is not enough in itself. We must accept restrictions to our freedom in both town and country, and it may well be that sophisticated methods of traffic control will have to be used as the number of motor vehicles increases. Parking restrictions —particularly on narrow lanes and in villages—are already common, and can be expected to increase. Some roads may have to be entirely closed to motor traffic and dedicated to horse riders and pedestrians. One way systems may be essential at peak times, and other roads may be developed into leisure drives for motorists. But certain wild and lonely areas between motor roads in Bowland, the Upper Dales and the North York Moors must be designated motorless or wilderness zones where it will be possible to be free from the sound and smell of the internal combustion engine. It may be necessary to ration parts of the countryside by discouraging too many people from going to the same place at once. Public transport will again come into its own; a cheap and fast rail or bus service from the city centre to the heart of the countryside may soon be much more acceptable than a traffic jam. Large car parks on the fringes of the best countryside could be served by mini-buses taking motorists from their cars into the remote areas. The drivers could act as guides and wardens, helping visitors to enjoy their day out.

What is most urgently needed is a comprehensive traffic and transport policy for the countryside—a rural Buchanan.

To Conclude

IN an age when transport to the moon has suddenly ceased to be science fiction it may seem absurd to assert that a humble little pack-horse way over a deserted Pennine moor is important. But it is. These islands have been inhabited now for upwards of ten thousand years. We live in an arrogant age with our space research, investigations into the structure of matter and even attempts to create life itself. We sometimes forget we are mere tenants of this planet and that what we destroy so thoughtlessly later ages may come to value. Yorkshire has so much that is precious. There are the obvious great works of architecture—York Minster, Fountains Abbey, Castle Howard and even Leeds and Bradford Town Halls. Transport has left us many fine monuments such as the old roads, the Leeds and Liverpool canal, and the viaducts of the Settle-Carlisle railway. It is possible too that later ages will develop means of transportation which will make the internal combustion engine and self-driven car as antiquated as the stage coach and the pack-horse. It could be that archaeologists a millenium hence will write scholarly papers on the origins and purposes of the Trans-Pennine Motorway!

But the smaller relics of our past—the pack-horse bridges, toll-booths, lock-keepers' cottages and village railway stations—are equally precious. The perspective of time these things give to our environment and our Yorkshire landscape is vitally important to us. Of course in town and country there must be progress, change and improvement, but it should be done by blending the present with what we most value of the past, thus creating in the landscape a sense of the depth of human history. Only if objects like the frail pack-horse bridge over Thorns Gill survive, shall we and our children and their children after them, be able to have any imaginative glimpse of what life was once like. Only then shall we be able to understand the past and ultimately understand ourselves.

A Selected Bibliography

General Background: *The Making of Modern Yorkshire* 1750-1914 by J. S. Fletcher (Allen & Unwin, 1918). *A History of Yorkshire* by W. Tate and F. Singleton (Davies Finlayson, 1960). *The Development of Transportation in Modern England* by W. J. Jackmann (new edit., Cass, 1962). *The Pennine Dales* by A. Raistrick (Eyre & Spottiswoode, 1968).

History of Roads and Road Transport: *The Rolling Road* by L. A. G. Strong (Hutchinson, 1956). *Great British Tramway Networks* by W. H. Bett and J. C. Gilham (Light Railway Transport League, 1957). *Pennine Journey* (also covers canals and railways) by W. B. Stocks (Advertiser Press, 1958). *The Tramways of Huddersfield* by R. Brook (Advertiser Press, 1959). *A Lancashire Lion* (history of Blackstone Edge pack-horse ways) by J. L. Maxim (Trustees of the late J. L. Maxim, Yorkshire Bank, Leeds, 1965). *Roads and their Traffic* 1750-1850 by J. Copeland (David & Charles, 1968). *Huddersfield Highways down the ages* by W. B. Crump (new edit., S. R. Publishers, 1969).

Navigations and Canals: *Inland Waterways of England* by L. T. C. Rolt (Allen & Unwin, 1950). *Cruising on the Leeds and Liverpool Canal* (British Waterways Board, 1966). *The Yorkshire Ouse* by Baron F. Duckham (David & Charles, 1967). *British Canals* by Charles Hadfield (new edit., David & Charles, 1969).

Railways: *The Midland Railway* by C. Hamilton Ellis (Ian Allan, 1952). *Great Central* by George Dow (Locomotive Publishing Co., 3 vols., 1959-65). *The Hull and Barnsley Railway* by G. D. Parkes (3rd edit., Oakwood Press, 1959). *The Railway King* (George Hudson) by R. S. Lambert (new edit., Allen & Unwin, 1964). *Regional History of the Railways of Great Britain: North-East England* by K. Hoole (David & Charles, 1965). *The History of the Great Northern Railway* by Charles H. Grinling (new edit., Allen & Unwin, 1966). *North of Leeds* by P. E. Baughan (Roundhouse, 1966). *The North Eastern Railway* by W. W. Tomlinson (new edit., David & Charles, 1967). *The Lancashire and Yorkshire Railway*, *Vol.* 1 by John Marshall (David & Charles, 1969). *The Railways of Wharfedale* by P. E. Baughan (David & Charles, 1969).

The Implications of the Motor Car: *The Re-shaping of British Railways* (Beeching Report) (British Railways Board, 1963). *The Rural Transport Problem* by David St. John Thomas (Routledge Kegan Paul, 1963). *Traffic in Towns* (shortened version of Buchanan Report) (Penguin, 1964). *Motor Traffic in the Craven Dales* (Craven Branch, C.P.R.E., 1965). *Man and Environment* by Robert Arvill (Penguin, 1967). *Leisure, Transport and Recreation* by David Rubinstein & Colin Speakman (Fabian Pamphlet No. 277, 1969).

Voluntary Organisations

A list of voluntary organisations concerned with aspects of transport history, preservation and amenity in Yorkshire. In each case write to the Secretary:

Footpaths, Bridleways, Green Lanes, etc.:
Commons, Open Spaces and Footpaths Preservation Society, 166 Shaftesbury Avenue, London W.C.2.
Council for the Preservation of Rural England, 4 Hobart Place, London S.W.1.
Peak and Northern Footpaths Society, 79 Taunton Road, Ashton-under-Lyne, Lancashire.
Ramblers' Association, 124 Finchley Road, London N.W.3.

Canals:
Inland Waterways Association, 114 Regent's Park Road, London N.W.1.
Pocklington Canal Amenity Society, 74 Westminster Road, York.

Railways:
Keighley and Worth Valley Railway Preservation Society, Haworth Station, Keighley.
Middleton Railway Trust, 12 Trelawn Crescent, Headingley, Leeds 6.
National Council on Inland Transport, 396 City Road, London E.C.1.
North Eastern Railway Association, Broughton House, West Ayton, Scarborough.
North Yorkshire Moors Railway Preservation Society, Rosebank, The Avenue, Ruswarp, Whitby.
Railway and Canal Historical Society, 14 Hobgate, York.
Railway Invigoration Society, 10 Grosvenor Gardens, Upminster, Essex.
Yorkshire Dales Railway Society, 17 Uplands, Skipton.

Tramways:
Light Railway Transport League, 14 Cudlow Avenue, Rustington, Sussex.

Industrial Archaeology:
North-East Industrial Archaeology Group, Bowes Museum, Barnard Castle, County Durham.
Teesside Industrial Archaeology Group, 15 Cromwell Terrace, Thornaby.

Museums of Industrial and Transport History:
Railway Museum, York (open weekdays only)
South Yorkshire Industrial Museum, Cusworth Hall, Doncaster.
Yorkshire Folk Museum, Shibden Hall, Halifax.

Index